To Andre,

with best wishes

from Mr Morel 1981.

KU-538-565

The Observer's Pocket Series

MUSIC

Observer's Books

The Observer's Book of

MUSIC

FREDA DINN
G.R.C.M., A.R.C.M.

ILLUSTRATED BY COLIN TWINN

WITH 8 COLOUR PLATES AND NUMEROUS
BLACK AND WHITE ILLUSTRATIONS

FREDERICK WARNE
LONDON

First published 1953 by
Frederick Warne & Co Ltd London
Copyright © Frederick Warne (Publishers) Ltd 1979

4th Edition 1979

ISBN 0 7232 1581 2

Printed in Great Britain by Butler & Tanner Ltd
Frome and London
0077·1178

CONTENTS

ACKNOWLEDGEMENTS

Our thanks are due to the following for allowing their instruments to be photographed by Traube Photography: Schott & Co Ltd for Plate 1, Boosey & Hawkes for Plates 2 and 3, The Early Music Shop for Plate 5 (lower) and Plate 8. Plate 4 is reproduced by courtesy of the Victoria and Albert Museum, Crown Copyright. Plate 5 (upper) and Plate 6 are reproduced by courtesy of the Donald Museum, Royal College of Music. Plate 7 was taken by A. F. Kersting.

LIST OF COLOUR PLATES

7

1 SOUND

We can enjoy music and at the same time have very little knowledge of its production. For most of us, however, some knowledge of the how and why of the production of musical sounds will not only have an interest for its own sake, but will also help to increase our enjoyment of music.

Let us imagine we are in a concert hall listening to an orchestra. What are the various steps in the process which begins with the effort expended by each player on his instrument and ends with our enjoyment of listening to the resultant sounds? The final question, why we should feel a sense of enjoyment in certain combinations of sounds, is a philosophical one and cannot concern us here. We can, however, say something about the mechanism of the sensation of sound.

We hear sound when our ear-drums are made to vibrate by disturbances in the air around us. These consist of a flow of alternating compressions and rarefactions of the air itself. A note of given pitch will be heard when the series of compressions and rarefactions follow each other in regular succession. When the succession of these 'vibrations' in the air has no regularity, a 'noise' and not a 'note' will be heard.

The speed at which sound travels is about 1100 feet (335·28 metres) per second. If we are in a very large hall, at the back, watching an orchestra as well as listening to it, it is likely that we shall hear the sounds from the orchestra fractionally after they appear to have been produced. Sound-waves can be reflected from hard surfaces, and their behaviour is not unlike that of light-waves. We find that there is more resonance from music performed in an empty hall than in one full of people, because we hear not only the sound coming direct from the instruments but also the reflections from the hard surfaces of walls and floor and empty seats. Such resonance is particularly noticeable in a cathedral or lofty church, and in no small measure adds to the 'ethereal' quality of the singing of a choir. In a concert hall the results can be much less pleasing, and there may be so much resonance that the music sounds blurred. Through advancement in the knowledge of acoustics and the availability of improved building materials, resonance can be controlled, as it has been, for example, in the construction of the Royal Festival Hall, London.

Sound-waves vary in two ways: in loudness and in pitch. The greater the agitation in the air, the louder

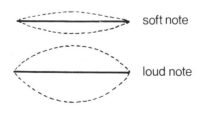

soft note

loud note

Soft and loud sound-waves

the sound; the amount of agitation is called the amplitude, and the degree of loudness is therefore determined by the degree of amplitude. The pitch of any note depends on the number of vibrations per second which reach the ear-drum: the more vibrations per second (the higher the frequency), the higher the pitch of the note; the fewer vibrations per second (the lower the frequency), the lower the pitch of the note. The first note we are likely to hear coming from the whole orchestra will be the tuning note, A, normally given by the oboe and 'tuned to' by all the pitched instruments of the orchestra. Instruments tuning to the pitch A:

will be producing a note having 440 vibrations per second. Some of the large instruments whose pitch-range is lower will tune to the A an octave below the oboe's A, which has 220 vibrations per second. It is likely that the piccolo, the smallest and therefore the highest-pitched instrument of the orchestra, will sound the A an octave above that of the oboe: the note will have 880 vibrations per second.

Here are the three As with their frequencies:

Each A has twice the number of vibrations per second of the A an octave below it; and, in fact, any note has twice the number of vibrations per second of the note an octave below it.

MAIN NOTES AND OVERTONES

The musical instrument, whatever its shape or size, is a device for setting the air into regular vibrations. It produces notes which are complex—that is, in addition to the main note that we hear and can name, there are other tones of higher frequency which vibrate within the note we consciously hear. Any note, therefore, consists of the lowest tone and a number of other tones, higher in pitch, that blend with it. The relative intensities of these various overtones fix the 'quality' or timbre of a note and they are responsible for the difference in tone-quality between, for instance, an oboe, a clarinet, a flute and a violin. The overtones conform to a definite pattern in relation to one another. The complete pattern is known as the harmonic series. With certain exceptions the possible overtones have frequencies which are in the ratio of 2, 3, 4, 5, 6, etc., to the lowest tone, the fundamental.

In musical notation the notes of the harmonic series are known as the *fundamental*, the *octave*, the *12th*, etc. Taking C as the fundamental the harmonic series is as follows:

(The notes in black are slightly flatter than those found on a keyboard.)

We may now begin to answer a question that will certainly occur to us while studying the orchestra: Why have the instruments such different shapes? And what are the general principles underlying the curious appearance of some of the instruments?

VIBRATORS AND RESONATORS

All musical instruments are made up of two parts: a *vibrator*, which the performer sets into motion, and a *resonator*, which serves to enhance the sound produced by the vibrator and to send the sound-waves into the air. In the violin family the string is the vibrator and the body of the violin, with its enclosed air, is the resonator. With a trumpet, the player's lips are the vibrator, and the air inside the tube of the trumpet is the resonator. However, different classes of instruments behave in different ways. First, there is the class of instrument in which the resonator will enhance notes throughout the pitch change and where the pitch of the note produced is determined by the rate of vibration set up. The string family—violin, viola, violoncello and double bass—are in this class. After the strings have been tuned by adjusting their tension (the greater the tension the higher the pitch), the pitch of the notes is determined by the position of the player's fingers on the strings—the shorter the vibrating portion of the string, the higher the pitch of the note. The actual sound produced from a vibrating string would not be resonant enough to be of any musical value, so the vibrations produced from the string are amplified and endowed with a particular tone-quality associated with instruments of the string family by the vibrations of the belly and back of the instrument and by the resounding cavity of air contained in its body. These vibrations communicate with the atmosphere through the wood and sound-holes of the instrument's belly. Furthermore, the individual tone-qualities of the violin, the viola, the violoncello and double bass are determined by these resonators.

The same principle of resonance applies to keyboard instruments with strings and to the harp. The

Kettle-drum

pitch is determined by the particular string set in vibration by being either struck, as in the pianoforte, or plucked, as in the harp. The resonance is provided by a thin sound-board, usually of pinewood.

The kettle-drum or timpano consists also of a vibrator (the stretched skin set in vibration by the player's stick) and a resonator (the air contained in the copper shell of the instrument).

Secondly, there is the class of instruments in which the resonator will enhance only certain notes, and once the vibrator has been set in motion its rate of vibration will be determined by the resonator itself. The woodwind and brass-wind instruments are in this class. When, for instance, a player blows across the mouth-hole of a flute, a stream of air from a narrow slit moves against the column of stagnant air and forms little eddies. The player blows against the sharp

14

A flautist

edge of the mouth-hole to coerce these eddies into order and to produce what is known as an 'edge-tone'. The stagnant air inside the flute is set in motion by the vibration of the edge-tone, and a note sounds, the pitch being determined by the length of the enclosed air-column.

If a pipe is closed at one end, as is the clarinet, the sounds made will be different, since the vibrations within the pipe will differ. The column of air travelling down the pipe will be reflected at the closed end and will again be reflected at the open end because of the elasticity of the surrounding air, and a series of waves will travel up and down the pipe. The pitch of the note will depend on the time taken for a compression to travel down the pipe and back again, that

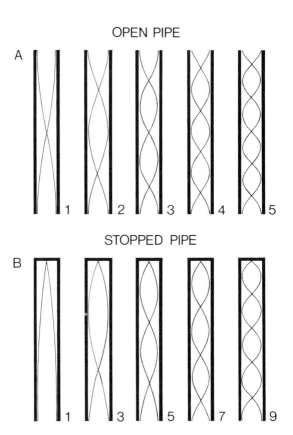

OPEN PIPE

A

1   2   3   4   5

STOPPED PIPE

B

1   3   5   7   9

Sub-divisions of a column of air in A, an open pipe,
and B, a stopped pipe

is, on the length of the pipe. These eddies in their travelling agitate the air in varying degrees. A point of greatest agitation is known as an antinode, and a point of least agitation is known as a node. At the 'stopped' or closed end of a pipe there is always a node, and at the open end—at the bell of an instrument, for instance—there is always an antinode.

A column of air in an open pipe can be made to vibrate in the sub-divisions shown in diagram A, while a column of air in a stopped pipe can be made to vibrate in the sub-divisions shown in diagram B.

Sound-waves formed in a stopped pipe can be longer than those formed in an open pipe of the same length and bore. The fundamental produced in a stopped pipe will therefore be lower in pitch than the fundamental produced in an open pipe. The sub-divisions or harmonics in a stopped pipe are limited, but in an open pipe all the harmonics are theoretically available.

Because of this, the first overtone of a clarinet, which is stopped at one end (the reed actually provides a closed end), is the 12th, while the first overtone of a flute, which is open at both ends, is the octave.

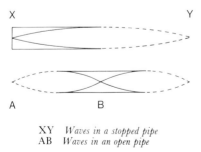

XY   *Waves in a stopped pipe*
AB   *Waves in an open pipe*

17

The oboe differs from the clarinet in that it has two reeds beating together instead of a single reed beating against a rigid 'table'. Also its tube is conical, instead of being cylindrical. By mathematical calculation it can be shown that the harmonics of a conical column closed at one end and open at the other are similar to those of a cylindrical column open at both ends: the full harmonic series is available. The complex note of the oboe has a 'reedy' tone, because the whole series of harmonics is contained in it, and some of them have a greater intensity than the fundamental. The tone of the clarinet has its particular quality because only the odd-numbered notes of the harmonic series are present.

The characteristic thinness of the tone of the flute was brought about by Theobald Boehm (1793 or 1794 to 1881) of Munich who gave the flute its present-day form and appearance. Although the main tube of the flute is cylindrical, there is, near the mouthpiece of the Boehm flute, a steady contraction of the bore towards the mouthpiece which causes the overtones to deviate from the harmonic series 2, 3, 4, etc., and because of this, they are not resonant and are called 'in-harmonic'. In this type of flute, therefore, the tone consists of little other than the fundamental.

In brass instruments the player's lips function in the same way as the double reed of an oboe. The player produces the note he wants by tightening his lips to get the higher notes, and holding them loose for the lower notes: his lips must vibrate at the same frequency as the note he requires. If the mouthpiece is cup-shaped the higher harmonics are formed, and the resultant tone is brilliant. If the mouthpiece is funnel-shaped, as on the horn, the tone will be more mellow, as the higher harmonics are not present.

If we want lower notes, we must have larger

resonators; if we want higher notes, we must have smaller resonators. It is for this reason that there are four different sizes of instruments in the string family: violin, viola, violoncello, double bass. Some of the brass instruments are many feet long, and obviously, if they were straight it would be impossible for the player to hold them, let alone carry them! This is why some brass instruments have such curious shapes. Of the woodwind family, the bassoon is the largest instrument, and its long tube is bent in such a way that it somewhat resembles a bundle of sticks—hence its Italian name, *fagotto*.

As the stringed instruments in an orchestra do not individually possess the same tone-power as the other instruments, there are always more of them, and they are always placed nearest to the audience. As most of the sound produced radiates from the bellies of stringed instruments, the orchestra is so arranged that as many string-players as possible have their instruments facing or sloping towards the audience.

The how and the why of the production of musical sounds have now been briefly described: more detail will be found later in this book, when each instrument is described.

Each player in an orchestra is chiefly concerned with playing the music put before him to the best of his ability. It is the conductor who is responsible for welding together all the separate parts into one complete whole, and he should be familiar with all the peculiarities, possibilities and shortcomings of the instruments in his orchestra so that he can get the best possible results from his players. A great deal of this work is done during rehearsals. At a performance the conductor should not only direct his players, but he should also inspire them so that listeners might fully enjoy the realization of the composer's vision.

2 MUSICAL INSTRUMENTS

STRINGED INSTRUMENTS

BOWED INSTRUMENTS

Nowadays, when we refer to the strings, we have in mind the violin family, consisting of four members: the violin, the viola, the violoncello (or cello) and the contra or double bass. These have many similar characteristics, but one of their chief differences is their size, ranging from the violin, the smallest, playing the highest notes, to the double bass, the largest, playing the lowest notes. The strings on all these instruments are normally set in vibration with a bow but are sometimes plucked with the fingers. As the quantity of tone is not as great from stringed instruments as from wind instruments, many more string players than wind players are required in an orchestra. In a large symphony orchestra there may be as many as 16 first violins, 14 second violins, 12 violas, 10 cellos and 8 double basses.

Violin The shape of the violin as we know it today emerged in Italy during the middle of the 16th century, having been gradually evolved from the rebec, a small bowed instrument of medieval times. The name 'violin' was applied to all the members of this family, and not only to the smallest one.

The French King Louis XIV had a band of 'twenty-four Violins' at his court, and Charles II on his return in 1660 set up a similar band in England. From this time the violin gained in popularity in England and that of the viol gradually waned.

The members of the violin family have many similar features which are shown in the diagram below. Their individual characteristics will be found in the descriptions in this chapter.

The sound is produced when the strings vibrate: the sound-waves travel through the bridge and sound post to the hollow body of the instrument which acts as a resonator, enhancing and amplifying them; they are then transmitted to the outside air through the sound-holes, back and belly.

The strings are tuned by tuning pegs: the greater the tension on the string the higher the pitch. The strings are said to be 'open' when they are sounded without the player's fingers placed upon them. Other notes are obtained by 'stopping': by pressing the strings with the fingers of the left hand to the finger-board, thus shortening their vibrating portion. The shorter the vibrating portion, the higher is the pitch

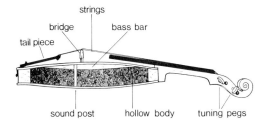

Longitudinal section of a violin

21

at the same tension and thickness of strings. Harmonics can be produced by touching the strings very lightly with the finger-tips (instead of 'stopping') at certain places. For example, if a string is touched at half its length, the octave above its 'open' pitch will sound; at a third of its length from either the bridge or the nut, the twelfth above will sound—and so on. On the lowest cello string these harmonics will sound.

Violin strings are made from the intestines of sheep cut in strips and then tightly twisted. The lower strings on the violin may be covered in fine metal wire (silver, copper or aluminium) in order to increase their resonance without adding to their length. Strings with a metal core are used by many players as they are more durable.

The table (or belly), bass bar, sound post, blocks and linings are made of pine; the back, ribs, neck and bridge are made of maple; the finger-board, tail-piece and nut are made of ebony; and the pegs are usually of rosewood. To prevent the wood from splitting across the body of the instrument after much use, and incidentally to enhance its appearance, a small groove is made near the edges of the belly and the back, into which three strips of lime-wood are inlaid. One is left light in colour, and the other two are stained black. This is known as purfling. Although the violin looks so delicate, it is carefully strengthened and reinforced inside with many small pieces of wood of various sizes. The body and neck are covered with many coats of special varnish to preserve the wood and to improve the tone as well as the appearance.

For special effect a mute can be placed on the bridge; this interferes with the transference of the vibrations to the interior of the violin and has the effect of dulling the upper harmonics, producing a nasal tone-quality.

By drawing the bow across the string the sound of the vibrating string can be sustained as in singing, and its sound can be varied in intensity by the skilled player. The bow consists of a stick which must be strong, yet flexible. Pernambuco wood and snake-wood from South America are both good—and the hair from the horse's tail, which is bleached for violin, viola and cello bows but left black for double bass. Today nylon is also used. By means of a screw the hair can be stretched for performance and slackened when not in use (to save the strain on the stick and the hair). When magnified, the hair shows 'thorns' as on a rose-briar, which, with the aid of powdered rosin or resin, grip the string and cause it to vibrate when the bow is drawn across parallel with the bridge. The violin bow has over 150 hairs.

The production and variation of tone are governed mainly by three factors: the distance of the bow on the string from the bridge; the pressure exerted on it; and the speed with which it travels over the string. The bow acquired its present shape towards the end of the 18th century when a more sprightly style of bowing was required. Its shape gradually changed (compare it with the viol bow), and its point of balance moved nearer to the heel, so that its weight, and therefore its strength, was transferred from the point to the heel. Today with the ever-increasing desire for musicians to give authentic performances of early music, the observant concert-goer will see original and reproduction bows in use; their shape and balance influence the tone produced on all the instruments of the violin family.

The modern violinist in a symphony orchestra holds his instrument between the left side of his chin and his collar-bone, so that his left hand is free to move along the neck of the violin and to stop the strings. The four strings are tuned in perfect 5ths, the lowest being G below middle C, the others D, A and E above. A skilled player can play as many notes as there are up to the top of the piano keyboard, but he cannot play anything below the G of his lowest string.

The terms 'first violin' and 'second violin' refer to the musical parts played, comparable with the first and second soprano voices in a choir. The instruments themselves are identical. In an orchestra the first violins are always on the left of the conductor so that their tone is directed towards the audience. The leader of the first violins is also known as the leader of the orchestra, and he is sometimes called upon to conduct. The second violins are either on the right of the conductor or more often on the left of the first violins. In chamber music (music for several instruments with one player to each part) the first violin always leads.

Viola   The viola is played in the same way as the violin, but as it is bigger it plays at a lower pitch. The strings are thicker and the bow is heavier. A great deal of its music is written in the alto clef, middle C being in the middle of the five lines, in order to avoid many leger lines and the constant changing between treble and bass clefs. Its normal pitch-range is from C below middle C extending upwards over three octaves.

Bass, alto, and treble clefs

Open strings

Violoncello (Cello) The cello is placed between the knees and is supported on the floor by an adjustable spike or endpin. The bow is shorter and heavier than the viola bow, and the strings are thicker and longer. They are tuned in perfect 5ths to C, G, D and A, an octave lower than those on the viola, the lowest string being two octaves below middle C. The cellist has to be familiar with three clefs: the bass, tenor and treble.

Bass, tenor, and treble clefs

When the left hand travels as far as the body of the cello, for the strings to be stopped in the higher positions, the thumb is used for stopping as well as the fingers. The cello tone can be sonorous, bright and clear, and its high notes can also have a cutting quality.

Double bass (Contrabass) This is a hybrid between the old violone and the violin family. It retains the characteristics of the viol in its shape, its tuning (in 4ths) and in its method of bowing. The double bass is a transposing instrument, that is, the notes sound an octave lower than written. The open strings are tuned to E, A, D and G, the E sounding E nearly two octaves below middle C (the E below the cello's C string).

Tromba marina A long, narrow medieval instrument with one string on which only the notes of the harmonic series are played. It sounds more like a wind instrument than a stringed one.

Rebec An early type of violin, the rebec came from the East and was in use throughout western Europe during the Middle Ages. It was known as the small fiddle in England, the *Geige* in Germany and the *gigue* in France. It is believed that the English dance, the jig, was so named from the instrument which provided the tune.

It is made from one piece of shaped wood (the neck being continuous with the body), part of which is hollowed out and then covered in with a flat board of pine-wood to make a resonator, like the body of the violin. It has three gut strings, tuned G, D, A and its tone is nasal and harsh in quality. Its descendant was the kit or pocket violin in England and the *pochette* in France. This was used by dancing-masters from the 17th century until the middle of the 19th century. It was so called because it could be carried, together with its small, dainty bow, in the coat pocket. During the Renaissance various sizes of rebec were in use, the bass and tenor being held between the knees, gambawise.

Viol There was a rudimentary form of viol as early as the 11th century. During the 15th century the viol was improved in Italy, where it acquired its present form and its six strings. It became popular for the performances of fancies and consorts. Because of the depth of its sides and the flatness of its back, the sound is soft, reedy and penetrating.

In England it acquired the name viol, and in Italy *viola de gamba* or leg-viol because it is held between

the legs. There are three usual sizes: the treble, tuned
thus:

the bass, tuned an octave lower, and the tenor or
mean, a 4th or 5th below the treble. A complete sett
or chest of viols, for home use, could include six viols,
two of each size.

Towards the end of the 17th century the division-
viol, a slightly smaller form of bass viol, became
popular for the performance of 'divisions' (variations
on a ground bass, or simple recurring melody). At
this time in England the smaller viols were being
ousted by the violins, but the bass viol survived for
nearly another 100 years. Viols are now being revived
both here and abroad, and they can be heard quite
frequently in performances of early music.

The violone, or double bass viol, was a large instrument playing an octave lower than the bass viol, and
was common in Italy and Germany (see double bass,
page 25).

The viol bow is different in shape from the modern
violin bow. The strongest part is at the point end,
whereas in the modern bow it is at the heel. There
is no ferrule, and the tension of the hair can be altered
by pressure of the fingers. All the viols are fretted with
gut, which is tied round the neck at each semitone.
To stop the strings, the fingers, placed immediately
behind the frets, press the strings towards the finger-
board, so that the vibrating portion of the strings is
between the bridge and the frets (not the fingers).
This gives a stopped note the sound quality of a note
played on an open string.

Viola d'amore

The *viola d'amore* is a tenor viol and is played like a violin. It usually has 14 strings: seven stopped and seven 'sympathetic' (which are made of fine steel or brass and pass under the finger-board and through the bridge; they vibrate 'in sympathy' with the stopped strings). There are many different tunings; the following is an example:

The stopped strings

The sympathetic strings

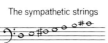

PLUCKED INSTRUMENTS

Harp It seems that the harp had its origin in prehistoric times, and might have developed from the stretched string of an archer's bow, other strings of varying length and pitch being added, much in the same way as reeds or whistles were bound together to make a syrinx or panpipes. The earliest evidence of a harp comes from Egypt and dates from the 13th century BC.

In the early years of Queen Victoria's reign, when drawing-room music was the fashion, it was not unusual for a young lady to play the harp, for it was an instrument warranted to display her airs and graces, both musical and non-musical, to the best advantage! With its triangular shape and gracefully curved neck, the harp is an elegant-looking instrument. The strings are plucked by the fingers, and the resultant vibrations are amplified by the sound-board. The frame is made of sycamore wood, the sound-board of pine. The pegs holding the lower ends of the strings are held in a strip of beech or other hard wood, which is glued along the centre of the sound-board. The tuning-pins, round which the upper ends of the strings are wound, pierce the wrest-plank which forms the upper part of the neck.

Most of the strings are of gut and some are coloured according to their pitch name to help the player to find them more easily. The eight lowest are either of metal or of silk over-spun with fine wire. The strings are tuned in the diatonic scale of C flat major, extending over six and a half octaves, from two octaves below

to two octaves above.

By a system of pedals each string can be raised in pitch by a half or a whole tone, e.g. all the C flats to C by moving the pedal one notch, and then to C sharp by moving it two notches. Chords and arpeggio figures sound well (*arpa* in Italian for harp), as does the swishing, swirling sound produced by sliding the fingers across the strings (known as a *glissando*).

The harp needs frequent tuning, and before an orchestral concert the harpist can often be seen tuning before the rest of the players have assembled.

Harpsichord The harpsichord was the most important of the keyboard instruments during the 16th, 17th and 18th centuries, holding a position analogous to that of the piano today. Three distinct instruments belong to the harpsichord family: the virginal (or virginals), the spinet and the harpsichord proper.

Fundamentally these instruments are like harps placed horizontally, with their strings plucked by plectra operated from a keyboard. When a key is depressed by the player's finger, a wooden jack rises, causing the plectrum (a quill or small piece of leather) to rise and pluck the string. When the key is released the jack falls, and the plectrum, which is fixed to a movable tongue of wood in the jack, slides silently past the string. When the jack comes to rest,

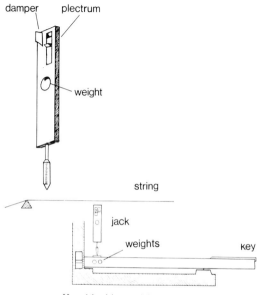

Harpsichord key, weights and jack

a small tongue of felt automatically damps the string
to stop it vibrating. (This jack is the origin of the term
'jack-in-the-box'.) Jacks are made of nylon in some
modern instruments. Metal strings are used, the
lower ones being over-spun with wire.

The harpsichord is the largest instrument in this
family. There are two or more strings to each note
and they run at right angles to the keyboard. The
compass of the harpsichord in the 16th century was
about four octaves from E in the 2nd octave below
middle C; this could be extended down to C by

retuning the E, F sharp and G sharp strings. By the second half of the 18th century some instruments, particularly those made by Jacob Kirkman in London, had a compass of five octaves from F in the 3rd octave below middle C. Some harpsichords have an additional set of strings sounding an octave higher.

To produce variety in tone-colour and resonance it is necessary to use mechanical devices, because so little difference can be made by finger-touch alone. By means of stops similar to those on an organ, or by pedals, the number of strings used to sound each note can be controlled. Similarly, the quality of tone can be changed to resemble that of a lute or a harp. In 1769 Tschudi (or Schudi) of London added the Venetian swell, which worked on the principle of the Venetian blind; this was operated by a pedal and could control the volume of sound by the opening and closing of shutters placed over the strings.

It seems that the double, or two-manual keyboard instrument was favoured in Britain and Germany, while the single manual was more popular in Italy. Today both types of harpsichord can frequently be heard. Many instruments have been carefully renovated and are being used as they were originally intended, no longer being silent museum specimens. New reproduction instruments are also being made by enthusiastic and highly skilled craftsmen who are carrying on the traditions of the 17th and 18th centuries.

Virginals   This was a favourite domestic instrument for ladies during the 16th and 17th centuries, hence its name; men preferred to play the lute. Towards the end of the 17th century it was superseded by the spinet and the larger harpsichord.

The virginals' case is rectangular and the strings run parallel with the keyboard. Each note has one

32

string, the sound is twangy, and no alteration in quality is possible. Its compass of four octaves could

be extended downwards by means of the short octave, the lowest G sharp being tuned to E, the F sharp to D, and the bottom note E to C. At the close of the 17th century a more complete chromatic compass was required, and some short-octave instruments can still be seen with the lowest G sharp and F sharp keys cut across, the back half giving the sharp and the front half the natural.

English virginals' music is of great importance in the history of music, as, together with the organ, it demonstrated some of the earliest developments of keyboard technique.

Up to the end of the 17th century the term 'virginals' was loosely used in Britain to refer to any instrument of the virginal, spinet or harpsichord family.

Spinet This is similar to the virginals in that it has one string to each note, but it is wing-shaped instead of rectangular. The strings run at an angle of about 45 degrees to the keyboard. It was a domestic instrument which was in use from the latter half of the 17th century to the end of the 18th century. No alteration in tone-quality is possible in performances.

Clavicytherium This is a vertical harpsichord. There is such an instrument in the Donald Museum at the RCM; it is considered to be the earliest specimen of a harpsichord in existence, having been made at the beginning of the 16th century.

Triangle (triang)   Today this small harpsichord is sometimes used, similar to the spinet, but with two pedals: the *crescendo*, which causes the strings to be plucked more strongly by the leather plectra, thus producing a louder tone; and the *harp*, which changes the tone-quality by damping the strings with felt. The legs are detachable and the instrument can be transported easily. The keyboard has a chromatic compass of five octaves:

Lute   The origin of the lute and other instruments with similar-shaped bodies, such as the rebec, mandore and mandoline, can be traced back into the distant past to the oriental type of instrument whose body was made from a gourd (or half-gourd) covered with a stretched skin. The name 'lute' comes from the Arabic words *El Oud*, meaning 'instrument of wood'.

By the 17th century the lute had acquired between 26 and 30 strings, and the tuning and adjusting of them was expensive both in time and money. During the 16th and 17th centuries it became very popular, and although it was the most difficult of plucked stringed instruments to play, much music was composed for it.

The strings of the lute are plucked with the fingers and are duplicated in unison. The vibrating length of string extends from the top of the finger-board to the sound-board; there is no bridge. The finger-board has frets of gut placed at each semitone, as on a viol. An elaborately carved disc of ivory or wood called the 'rose', is usually inserted in the circular sound-hole. The sound-board is of pine-wood, and

34

the pear-shaped back is made from fine strips of English maple, or sometimes from ivory and ebony, which are glued together.

Archlute   The largest member of the lute family, the archlute, has a double peg-box, so that some of the strings are not over the finger-board and can only be played as open strings. The theorbo is similar to the archlute, but smaller.

A special notation called 'tablature' was used for all lute music, showing diagrammatically the string and fret to be used for each note, with its duration indicated above by small marks similar to the tails of modern staff notation.

Mandore (Mandora)   The smallest lute, the mandore (or mandora), was used by the travelling minstrels in Europe from the 12th to the 14th centuries, and there is evidence of its use in England during the 15th century. At this time another easily portable instrument developed; this form survives as the mandoline.

Mandoline   This has a pear-shaped body similar to the lute. The frets and strings are of metal. The eight strings are tuned in pairs to G, D, A and E, as on the violin. They are plucked with a plectrum of tortoiseshell held between the thumb and first finger of the right hand.

Cittern   This was a popular instrument during the 15th century, but it was ousted by the superior attractions of the lute. Later it could frequently be found hanging in taverns and barbers' shops for the amusement of waiting customers. The strings of metal are tuned in pairs and are plucked with the fingers. Music for it was printed in tablature.

Guitar   This is of great antiquity, having originally

come to Europe through the Moors in Spain. The Spanish guitar, popular today, is a direct descendant of the lute and cittern. Its flat back and sides are made of maple, ash, service or cherry-wood; its sound-board, with a decorative sound-hole, is of pine; and its neck and finger-board are of some hard wood, such as ebony, pear-wood or beech. The finger-board has metal frets placed at intervals of a semitone. Metal screws instead of rosewood pegs are used for tuning the strings, of which there are six: normally three of gut and three of silk over-spun with silver wire. Today some of the upper strings may be made of nylon. The guitar is tuned thus:

but the notes are written thus:

To facilitate fingering in remote keys, the *capo-tasto*, or *cejuela*, may be clamped on the finger-board; it raises the pitch of all the open strings.

HIT INSTRUMENTS

Pianoforte About the year 1709 Cristofori, in Florence, produced a *gravicembalo col piano e forte*—'a harpsichord with soft and loud'. In this instrument the strings were not plucked but were hit by hammers. The loudness and softness of the notes could be directly controlled by the amount of force exerted by the player's fingers on the keys. Earlier attempts at creating such an instrument had been made, but the

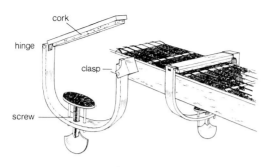

Capo tasto

new principle was not established until the production of Cristofori's instruments.

At the beginning of the 18th century there were two main kinds of domestic keyboard instruments, the harpsichord and the clavichord (which, despite its very small tone, had considerable qualities of expression). Through the desire to combine the tone of the harpsichord with the less mechanical and more expressive qualities of the clavichord, the pianoforte evolved.

By the middle of the 18th century the square piano was produced and it quickly became very popular. In size and shape it was like the virginals. Some models were made to look like tables and were fitted with drawers to hold music.

At the beginning of the 19th century the familiar upright piano was produced. In this kind of instrument the strings are mounted on a metal frame in a plane at right angles to the keyboard and they extend below the level of the keyboard. Today several sizes of piano are in use, ranging from the upright, which occupies the least floor space, through the baby grand, only four feet long, to the full concert grand, which is eight and a half feet long. Many experiments and improvements were made in the construction of the piano, but it was not recognized as an independent instrument until the end of the 18th and the beginning of the 19th centuries, when composers such as Beethoven and Schubert were writing specially for it.

If the panel immediately above the keyboard of an upright piano is removed, it will be seen that when the finger presses a key it brings a felt-covered hammer into operation. This immediately moves forward, strikes the strings and then quickly rebounds. A small felt pad, the damper, which normally presses

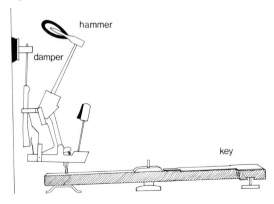

Action in upright piano

on the strings, is released at the moment of striking, so that the strings are allowed to vibrate freely until they come to rest, or until the finger releases the key, which immediately returns the damper to the string. All this mechanism is called the 'action'. The sound is similarly produced in a grand piano, but on a horizontal plane, with the hammers hitting the strings from below.

If the lower panel under the keyboard of an upright piano is removed, the iron frame will be seen, on which the metal strings are stretched. They are fixed at their top ends to tuning-pins, which the tuner turns with a tuning-hammer when he restores the strings to their correct pitch. Behind the strings is a varnished board; it is of very thin pine and is the sound-board or resonator, amplifying the sound of the strings and enhancing their tone-quality.

The shorter, thinner strings on the right-hand side produce the higher, or treble notes; those on the left-hand side are longer and thicker for producing the lower, or bass notes. There are three strings to each of the higher notes, because one or two would be insufficient to produce the required amount of tone; then two to each of the lower notes; and finally only one to each of the notes in the extreme bass. The low strings are over-spun with thick wire; if they were not, they would need to be very much longer to produce the low notes with enough resonance.

When the sustaining pedal on the right is pressed down, all the dampers are released from the strings which then continue to vibrate after they have been struck. When the left pedal on an upright piano is pressed down, the hammers are moved closer to the strings so that they strike with less force; in a grand piano the hammers are automatically shifted sideways, so that only one string out of three is struck. Hence the terms, *una corda* ('one string') when the

left pedal is depressed and *tre corde* ('three strings')
when it is released.

The normal compass of a piano is seven or seven
and a quarter octaves, extending from two octaves
below to two octaves above middle C.

Clavichord   The clavichord is contained in a rectangular box with the strings running parallel with the
keyboard. Each string is made to sound not by a plectrum, as in the harpsichord type of instruments, but
by a metal tangent which hits the string and presses
against it. On hitting the string, the tangent divides
it into two lengths, one of which is free to vibrate
while the other is permanently damped by a piece
of felt. The tangent thus sets the string in vibration,
and the pitch of the note is determined by the point
on the string where the tangent hits it, thus stopping
the string and having the same effect on it as the
player's left-hand fingers have on the strings of a
violin or guitar or any other similar instrument.

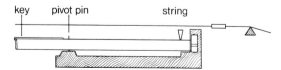

Clavichord action

In clavichords made before about 1725 one string was made to serve two or more adjacent keys, thus economizing on the number of strings needed. Such an arrangement was possible by the respective tangents for these adjacent keys being placed along the same string. These adjacent notes could not, of course, be sounded together, but then they were rarely needed. Clavichords of this type were called 'fretted' in England and *gebunden* (bound) in Germany.

The tone-quality of the clavichord is small and delicate. By agitating the depressed key, a kind of vibrato, known as *Bebung*, can be produced, whereby a note can be prolonged. The clavichord is the only stringed keyboard instrument on which such an effect is possible.

The clavichord was popular from about the 15th century to the beginning of the 19th century, when it gave place to the pianoforte. In Bach's time its compass was from two octaves below middle C to two octaves above middle C. Interest in its revival is now growing, and some very fine instruments are being made and played.

Dulcimer   This is a shallow, closed wooden box strung with wires which are hit with small wooden hammers. It was used mostly in puppet plays in the 17th and 18th centuries in England, but there is also mention of it in English literature as early as the 15th century. Today it is played by gipsy musicians in eastern Europe, where it is called the 'cymbalum' or 'zimbalon'.

Psaltery   A very old instrument, the psaltery is similar to the dulcimer but the strings are plucked with the fingers or with a plectrum. Known as the 'kin' in China, it has existed there for thousands of years. The many-stringed psaltery found its way westward into Europe from Asia Minor and was known during the Middle Ages by many other names, including 'cythera barbarica'.

It might be said that the dulcimer, with its hit strings was the forerunner of the pianoforte, while the psaltery, with plucked strings, was the forerunner of the harpsichord.

Zither   This is an elaborate kind of psaltery played in the Tyrol and adjoining mountainous districts. The player places it on a table and stops some of the strings with his left thumb, plucking a melody on them with a plectrum on his right thumb, while playing an accompaniment on some of the other strings with the fingers of his right hand.

Hurdy-gurdy   This is a stringed instrument of the violin type. The strings are set in vibration by a resined wooden wheel, turned by the player's right hand, while the fingers of his left hand press keys, not unlike those of the piano, to stop the strings. Of the six strings, the two outside ones are tuned to the keynote of the piece and sound continuously, thus forming a drone.

All wind instruments are made to sound by causing air to vibrate inside a hollow tube. Part of this tube must be open so that the air inside it has contact with the surrounding air. The inside of the instrument, known as the bore, may be cylindrical (the same width throughout its length) or conical (small at one end and gradually increasing in width towards the other), or it may be cylindrical for part of its length and conical for the remainder. The tube may be straight or curved.

The choice of material for a wind instrument depends on a number of factors, such as its ability to withstand the strain imposed on it by various processes during manufacture, its durability, its flexibility and its weight. The finished instrument must be hard and rigid, and the inside of the tube must be smooth.

Wind instruments were played in ancient times: remains of bone flutes of the later Stone Age have been found. We know from the Bible that a flute-like instrument was played in Hebrew religious processions, with drums, tambourines and cymbals, and that a ram's horn was blown on special occasions. Over 3000 years ago the Egyptians used trumpets on ceremonial occasions, and later the Greeks held contests at the Pythian games for solo playing on the aulos, a double-reed instrument related to the oboe. The Romans, too, had a kind of oboe, and trumpet-like instruments of different sizes. Since early times wind instruments have been gradually modified and improved, and are continually being developed and extended to suit the demands of contemporary composers and players.

Wind instruments are divided into two classes, the woodwind and the brass. The term 'woodwind' does not signify that all the instruments in this class are made of wood; some are of ivory, metal, and ebonite. Nor does the term 'brass' mean that all these instruments are made of brass; there are some of silver, copper, horn, ivory and even wood. The families of instruments generally regarded as woodwind are the flute, oboe, clarinet, saxophone and bassoon. The brass are horns, trumpets, cornets, trombones and tubas.

This classification is based on the method of producing the sound. A generator must be used to set the air in vibration. There are three types of generators: the free air-reed, the cane-reed and the lip-reed. If the sound is generated by air-reeds, as in the flute, or cane-reeds, as in the oboe and clarinet, the instrument is defined as 'woodwind'; if the sound is generated by the vibration of the lips against a cup-shaped or conical mouthpiece, the instrument is defined as 'brass'.

With the free air-reed, a compressed stream of air from the player's lips is blown against the edge of a mouth-hole (the embouchure) in the upper side of the tube. Transverse flutes, piccolos and fifes are played in this way. Instead of the air-stream being directed straight from the player's mouth on to a mouth-hole, it can be driven through a channel in a beak-shaped mouthpiece and directed automatically against the sharp edge of the sound-hole. Recorders, flageolets and tin whistles are played in this way.

The cane-reed may be a double or single reed. The double reed, used for playing the oboe, cor anglais and bassoon, consists of two small pieces of cane shaved thin at one end. At the thicker end they are bound together over a small metal tube called the staple. The paper-thin ends of the reeds are pressed flat almost together, but a small gap is left between

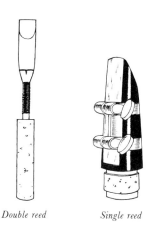

Double reed   *Single reed*

them, which is made narrower by the player's lips
when he sets the reeds in vibration by blowing
through them. The lower part of the staple is larger
and it is covered in cork so that it fits tightly into the
top of the instrument. The staple is replaced by the
crook in the bassoon. The single reed is a flat
piece of cane shaved thin at one end. The thicker
end is clamped by the ligature to the flat side of a
beak-shaped mouthpiece. The thinner end lies over
a narrow channel in the mouthpiece so that the reed
can vibrate when the player forces a stream of air
between the reed and the mouthpiece.

With the lip-reed the almost closed lips of the
player vibrate like reeds against a cup- or cone-
shaped mouthpiece. The vibration is conveyed to the
air in the tube of the instrument through the throat
or neck of the mouthpiece. The quality of the tone

Deep mouthpiece   *Shallow mouthpiece*

produced depends on the shape of the mouthpiece; for instance, a brassy, bright tone is produced from a shallow cup, while a more mellow, veiled tone requires a deep cone. The smaller the mouthpiece in circumference, the higher the sounds which can be easily produced.

On a wind instrument the pitch of the sound is determined by the frequency (or rate) of vibrations that are set up in the column of air contained within the tube of the instrument. It is a natural law that a column of air of a fixed length can be made to vibrate at certain frequencies only. This means that only one series of sounds can be produced from a column of air of a fixed length.

The wind-player can produce these sounds by varying the intensity of the air-stream. This he does by varying the pressure of his lips; the more he tightens them, the more compressed the air-stream will be, increasing the rate of vibration and so producing notes of higher pitch. The player slackens his lips in order to produce notes of lower pitch. The lowest possible note he can produce from a tube is the fundamental; the higher ones—the octave, 12th, double octave and so on—are known as the 'harmonics'.

The following 'harmonic series' of notes can be produced by the lips on a tube without side-holes, of about eight feet long (black notes indicate pitches very slightly flatter than written):

If the tube were shorter, the sounds would all be relatively higher, so that a tube about four feet long would produce the following sounds:

If the tube were longer, about eight and a half feet, these sounds would be available:

An entire harmonic series is contained within any tube, but it is not humanly possible to produce all the notes, because of the great lip-pressure needed. The width of the tube in proportion to its length is the factor determining the number of playable sounds. A wide-bored tube will sound its fundamental easily and, if it is not too wide, some of the lower harmonics as well. A narrower-bored tube might not sound the lowest two notes but it will sound the higher ones up to the 16th note of the series.

The woodwind instruments are wide in bore compared with their length, and only the fundamental and octave, or, as in the clarinet, the fundamental and 12th sound easily. The brass instruments are narrow in bore compared with their length, and so the middle and higher harmonics are easier to produce. This is one of the essential differences between woodwind and brass instruments.

The number of playable sounds that can be produced without side-holes on a woodwind instrument is therefore very limited. If however a side-hole is bored in the tube, the sounding-length is shortened, as the presence of the hole has approximately the same effect as cutting off the length of the tube at the position of the hole. By having a number of holes that can be covered by the fingers, the sounding-length can be varied by the player. The shorter the tube, the higher the pitch of the fundamental will be. The octave above these fundamental notes can be obtained by the player using the same fingering but blowing harder, except on the clarinet which, because of its shape (see page 53), sounds the 12th instead of the octave.

WOODWIND INSTRUMENTS

Flute, piccolo   The flute and piccolo are the only orchestral wind instruments held sideways. The *flauto piccolo*, the small flute, to give it its full name, is the smallest instrument in the orchestra. It has a bright, piercing tone and is usually used for some particularly

Flute   *Piccolo*

brilliant sound effect. As it is not always required, one of the two or three flautists will play it when he is not required on the flute.

One flute can hold its own quite easily against all the strings in the orchestra, and for this reason it is a solo orchestral instrument. Usually there are two flutes, each playing his own part but occasionally they 'double', both playing the same part. The flute has a pitch-range of three octaves from middle C upwards. The piccolo has a range of two octaves and five notes from the D an octave and one note above middle C, but experienced players can play one or two notes higher. The flute and piccolo are normally made of silver-based metal, but sometimes of wood; the flute is jointed in three sections.

Oboe All the instruments of the oboe family are of conical bore and have a double reed. The oboe has a compass from B flat below middle C to the F two octaves and a 4th above. The instrument, of African blackwood or ebonite, is made in three sections: the top joint, into which the staple carrying the reed is inserted, the middle joint and the bell-joint. There are usually two oboes in a symphony orchestra, either playing different parts or doubling in the same way as the flutes. Their tone is penetrating and reedy, which can be particularly expressive when the player uses vibrato.

Cor anglais (English horn) This is neither English nor a horn, but an oboe larger than the concert oboe and sounding a 5th lower. The name is a corruption of *cor anglé* ('angled horn'), so called because of the crook into which the double reed is inserted. The instrument is longer than the oboe and it has a globular or pear-shaped bell. The tone is rather melancholy. Like the piccolo, this is an extra instrument which is not constantly used in the symphony orchestra; when needed it is played by an oboe player.

Bassoon This is so called as it was regarded as a bass instrument to the oboe. In Italy it is known as *fagotto*, and in Germany *Fagott* because its long, bent

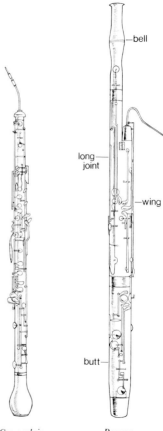

bell

long
joint

wing

butt

Oboe   *Cor anglais*   *Bassoon*

51

tube resembles a bundle of sticks. As it is over two metres long the tube has to be bent back on itself so that the player can reach the finger-holes. There are four sections of wood which fit tightly together—the wing, the butt, the long joint and the bell. The double reed is inserted into the crook. The bassoon plays the bass part in any woodwind quartet under the flute, oboe and clarinet. It has a compass from the B flat, a 9th below middle C to the F an octave and a half above middle C. The double bassoon plays one octave below the bassoon. It is not a regular member of the orchestra.

In its earliest form, during the 16th century, the bassoon was known as the curtal. Two connective channels were bored in one piece of wood, with a brass crook for the reed at the top end of one and a narrow bell at the top of the other.

Shawm   This is the forerunner of the modern double reed orchestral instrument. Shawms are loud, outdoor instruments of various sizes often played in an ensemble; they are of early medieval origin and were played with trumpets and drums in military bands at the time of the crusades.

Clarinet   The clarinet consists of a cylindrical tube with a single beating reed. The tone is less nasal than that of the oboe. Since the reed effectively closes one end of the tube the pipe is stopped, and thus produces notes an octave lower than those from an open pipe of the same length (see Chapter 1). The orchestral clarinet has a notational compass of nearly four octaves from E in the bass stave upwards. In a symphony orchestra the clarinettist usually has two instruments, one in A and another in B flat. (They are transposing instruments.) The clarinet in C is not normally used as its tone is inferior to the others, but it is used in military bands and occasionally in the

Clarinet   *Bass clarinet*

orchestra for a special effect. With modern techniques and instruments clarinettists generally need to use only the B flat instrument. Mozart was the first of the great composers to introduce the clarinet into the orchestra, in his Paris Symphony (1778), after having heard it earlier in that year in Stamitz's orchestra at Mannheim.

Bass clarinet   This is usually in B flat, plays an octave lower than the clarinet. As it has such a long tube, the lower portion of it is curved upwards and ends in a bell, and the upper end is bent downwards so that the reed is within reach of the player's mouth. The bass clarinet is not a regular member of the orchestra.

Basset horn   This is a tenor instrument which looks like the bass clarinet. It plays a 4th below a B flat clarinet and has an extended range down to the F two and a half octaves below middle C. Mozart and Richard Strauss scored for this instrument in some of their works.

Saxophone   Adolphe Sax of Brussels invented the saxophone in 1840. It is made of metal, has a single reed like the clarinet and a conical bore like the oboe. Two instruments are in general use today: one is in B flat, the other in E flat. They are both transposing instruments (see page 136). The saxophone is not a regular member of the symphony orchestra but many composers, including Mahler, Debussy, Richard Strauss, Hindemith and Vaughan Williams, wrote music for it, and composers today continue to do so, using it orchestrally and as a solo instrument. Instruments of the saxophone family (soprano, alto and tenor) are most commonly found in jazz bands.

Saxophone

Horn   The orchestral horn is known as the 'French horn'. It is a brass instrument with a narrow, conical tube, over 11 feet (3·4 metres) long, ending in a large bell and with a funnel-shaped mouthpiece. There are two types of French horn: the older natural or hand horn, and the more modern valve horn. The notes of the harmonic series are available on brass instruments, but as the bore of the horn tube is so narrow compared with its length, it is impossible to produce the fundamental with any resonance of musical value.

Originally the horn was actually an animal horn; later it still maintained its curved cone shape although it could be made of any hard substance. It was used mainly for signalling of various kinds, for ceremonies and for rituals in the Middle Ages. The later hunting horns were much longer; more notes could be blown on them, and they were made circular so that they were easier to carry on the hunting field.

Early in the 18th century the 'natural' hunting horn was adopted into the orchestra. To increase the range of available notes, pieces of tubing of various lengths known as crooks were inserted into the tube; the total length of the vibrating air-column could be altered, changing the pitch of the fundamental and the corresponding harmonic series above it and thus making different notes available. Contemporary orchestral parts show that horns in G, F, E flat, D and C could be required. By inserting either the G, F, E flat, D or C crooks into the instrument, therefore, the corresponding harmonic series above each of these fundamentals could be sounded by the player on one instrument, obviating the need for a horn in each of these keys. All horn parts were written in the key of C, and the treble clef was used except

for those notes that extended into the bass clef, and
these were written an octave lower than they
sounded. The notes available on the natural horn in
C alto were:

The notes available on the natural horn in F were:

A complete scale was not possible on the natural
horn, and some notes were out of tune with the
tempered scale, but the player could adjust the pitch
of these sounds by inserting his right hand into the
bell of the instrument; these notes are known as
stopped notes.

The French horn with valves is the one now used
in the orchestra. Normally it is pitched in F. By means
of valves, all the notes of the chromatic scale not available in the natural harmonic series can be provided.
Operated by three fingers of the player's left hand,
the valves instantaneously bring into use pieces of
tubing that lengthen the air-column by a semitone,
two semitones or three semitones respectively; as
these valves can be used simultaneously, the air-
column can be extended as much as six semitones.
Thus the valves fulfil the same function as crooks but
are faster and more efficient to use. For example, by
playing the third harmonic 'naturally' the player can
get any of the six notes beneath it by means of his
valves.

The valve system was invented during the second
decade of the 19th century, but the natural horn held

its own until about the middle of the century. For some years both forms were used in the orchestra, but the natural horn had finally disappeared by the last quarter of the century. The early valve horns were far from perfect, and for this reason they were ignored by composers until about 1835. Some Prussian military bands, however, adopted them before 1830.

The German double horn, which can, by means of a valve, be played in either F or B flat alto, is gaining in popularity; the B flat alto form is favoured for the production of higher notes.

The tone of the horns can be rich, rounded and mellow and they blend well with the woodwind. The tone can be subdued by the insertion of a mute into the bell and can be made harsh by harder blowing. In the symphony orchestra four horns are normally used, although some late 19th-century works require more.

Trumpet   The trumpet consists of a narrow tube, cylindrical for most of its length; it ends in a bell of medium size and has a cup-shaped mouthpiece. Its compass is higher than that of the horn and the tone is brighter. Like the horn, there are two main types of trumpet—the natural trumpet (with crook) and the modern valve trumpet.

The history of the trumpet goes back to ancient times, and it played an important part in early religious ceremonies, such as those described in the Bible. There is evidence that it was also used in battle by the Greeks and in procession by the Romans. Henry VIII had 42 instrumentalists, of whom 14 were trumpeters.

The natural trumpet became a member of the orchestra at the beginning of the 17th century, and Purcell, Bach and Handel wrote florid solo parts for it. In the works of Haydn and Mozart it became

58

much less a melodic instrument, and the higher notes were no longer used. The natural trumpet with crooks was used in orchestras until well into the 19th century.

The modern valve trumpet used in today's orchestra is played on the same principle as the valve horn. It is pitched in B flat, but can be altered to A by a rotary change valve. It is four and a half feet long, only half the length of the old natural trumpet. There are usually three trumpets in a symphony orchestra. The natural trumpet without crooks is now only used in England for ceremonial fanfares.

Bach trumpet   Fewer crooks were used in Bach's time than later on; every orchestral trumpet player would have to have four trumpets by his side—in G, F, D and B flat. By means of crooks the player could lower the pitch of these trumpets a tone or a semitone, and in some cases, by muting, he could raise the pitch a semitone. Thus he could play in any key, but he could play only the sounds of the harmonic series within that key.

The instruments then in use were twice as long as those used today, and the player was expected to be able to produce notes in the fourth octave, where the harmonics lie scale-wise, as well as the lower harmonic sounds such as the third to the eighth. These high sounds (clarino parts) were not easy to play; they required much practice and hard work, even for the most skilled and experienced player.

During the 19th century trumpet players were favouring a shorter instrument. Interest in Bach's music was increasing, but players had lost the art of playing the higher notes that had been reached on the old, long trumpet, and they found clarino parts very difficult to play on their own instruments. In 1884 a straightened valve trumpet with a conical

The actual fundamentals are not as easy to produce as the harmonics; they are spoken of as 'pedal notes', and are seldom if ever used on the bass trombone.

Cornet　The cornet consists of a metal tube which is for the most part cylindrical in bore and for the rest conical. It has a cup-shaped mouthpiece, which is usually deeper than that of a trumpet. Its compass is almost the same as that of the trumpet, and the gaps of the harmonic series are filled in by means of three valves. As the bore of the cornet is wider than that of the trumpet, the production of the notes is easier, and therefore greater flexibility in performance is possible. The tone has neither the brilliance of the trumpet nor the mellowness of the horn.

Nowadays the cornet is in B flat, but it can automatically be changed to A by opening an extra short length of tubing.

The cornet was introduced in France in about 1827. It was a development of the small horn that was known by several names, such as *cornet simple, cornet de poste* or *cornet ordinaire*. Originally the cornet was about 4 ft (1·2 m) long and was in C, but by means of coiled crooks it could be lowered in pitch by one, two, three or four semitones. The only attainable notes of the harmonic series were 2, 3, 4, 5, 6, 7 and 8. Since 1827 many alterations in the shape of the cornet have been made, but during the last 50 years very little change has taken place. Because of the comparative ease with which it can be played, the cornet has been adopted in most European countries for use in military bands, brass bands and light orchestral music; it is not normally used in the symphony orchestra.

Bugle　This is used mainly for military signalling. It consists of a brass or copper tube with wide conical bore, ending in a bell and with a cup-shaped mouthpiece. With these characteristics it is therefore related

to the horn and the trumpet, but because it has no
keys or valves only a few notes of the harmonic series
are playable.

Tuba   The name 'tuba' is an omnibus word now
used for any brass instrument, other than the trombones, that can play a bass part.

Neither the horn nor the trumpet can sound the
fundamental note because of their narrow bore. This
means, for instance, that for a horn in C to sound its
bottom note, the second harmonic

(known as the '8 foot C'), the length of its tube must
be 16 feet (4·8 metres), and thus half its length is prac-
tically useless. When experiments on brass instrument valves were being made it was found that if the
conical bore of a tube were made wide enough in proportion to its length, the fundamental note could be
played when a cup-shaped mouthpiece was used.
This knowledge opened up many possibilities.

The Germans classified brass instruments into half-
tube and whole-tube instruments. The first were
those with narrow bore, lacking the fundamental
note, such as horns and trumpets; the second, the
whole-tube instruments, were those with a wide bore
and a playable fundamental note, such as tubas. On
the half-tube instruments it was found that only three
valves were needed for filling in the missing notes
between the notes of the harmonic series, but on the
whole-tube instruments there was a bigger gap to fill
between the first and second harmonic; it was therefore necessary to add a fourth valve, which, used on
its own, would lower the pitch by two and a half tones
and, in conjunction with the other three, would fill

in an entire octave, the distance between the first and second harmonics.

The tuba used in the orchestra today is far from being a standardized instrument. In this country it is built in F, and is a development of the military E flat tuba. It has a compass of

8va basso

and is used to supply the lowest notes in the brass section of the orchestra. Its tone can be dignified and pompous, and it can also sound comic.

EARLY WIND INSTRUMENTS

Apart from those mentioned above (shawm, curtal, etc.) a number of other, less familiar early instruments have come into use with the revival of early music (see page 171).

Cornamuse A straight, wooden, double-reed wind-cap instrument with strident tone, sounding an octave lower than the crumhorn. Several sizes exist.

Cornett A woodwind instrument with a cup-shaped mouthpiece, originally made from cow horn but later from wood. It has a brilliant trumpet-like tone and was often played outdoors in consort with sackbuts.

Crumhorn This is a narrow-bored instrument, originally made of boxwood, with the lower end bent round. It has a double reed enclosed in a wind cap: the reed does not touch the player's lips but responds to the pressure of the air blown through the cap. This was the most popular double-reed wind-cap instrument from the 15th century to the 17th. Several sizes exist.

Gemshorn This is a medieval type of folk recorder, with a small pitch-range and a clear, ocarina-like tone. Gemshorns were originally made from the horn of the gem, a wild mountain antelope.

Rackett This is a double-reed, multiple-bored Renaissance and Baroque instrument which exists in many sizes. They are all relatively short and squat, and have a penetrating nasal tone and low pitch-range.

Rauschpfeife This is a straight, wooden wind-cap instrument with loud tone, sounding rather like a shawm.

Serpent This is the bass instrument of the cornet family and is made of wood and covered in leather. The long, sectional tube forms three U-bends and ends in an almost complete circle with the open end pointing upwards. From about 1500 to 1650 it was used for all kinds of indoor and outdoor music. It should not be confused with the 19th-century orchestral serpent, now obsolete.

Sordun This is a Renaissance type of bassoon, made from one piece of wood with a cylindrical bore and sounding an octave lower than the written notes. Several different sizes of sordun may be played together and in consort with recorders.

PERCUSSION INSTRUMENTS

Percussion instruments are members of an ancient instrumental family—perhaps the oldest. Some of its members still retain their primitive form in the modern orchestra.

Percussion instruments are mentioned in the Bible and have always been popular in Asia and Africa; instruments from these continents have found their way into Europe at different periods in history. It seems that during the 12th, 13th and 14th centuries the crusades were responsible for bringing the kettle-drums (then called nakers) to Europe. During the 18th century the popularity in European armies of 'Turkish music' introduced via Austro-Hungary caused the addition of a variety of percussion instruments. In the 20th century, with the influence of American negro music and jazz on dance music, further additions have been made.

DRUMS

These are made of a skin stretched over a frame. There are several kinds of drum used in the symphony orchestra: the kettle-drum, the side-drum, the bass drum and the tenor drum; the tambourine is also a form of drum.

Kettle-drums (timpani) These are the only drums that can produce notes of definite pitch. A wooden hoop over which a skin is stretched is held in place by a circular iron ring mounted on a basin-shaped metal shell. By means of screws or taps placed round the shell, the tension on the skin can be adjusted for tuning the drum. The more modern pedal timpani can be tuned by a pedal during performance; a *glissando* effect can also be made in this way.

Kettle-drum, new version

Drum-sticks of cane, with padded ends ('heads'), are used for hitting the drum to produce the sound. Sometimes side-drum sticks or sponge-headed sticks are used for special effects.

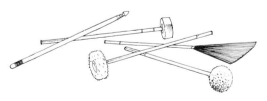

Drum-sticks

Two kettle-drums were used in the 18th-century orchestra, the larger drum with the range:

and the smaller

As only one note could be obtained on each drum without retuning, the notes chosen were usually the tonic (*doh*) and the dominant (*soh*) of the key of the composition. After Beethoven's day, however, any pair of notes might be used. During the 19th century three drums became the usual number required by composers, with the following pitch-range:

Other sizes have since been required for the performance of certain works, but they are exceptional. The low, middle and high drums are those which are normally in use today. The introduction of pedal timpani has increased the range of available notes.

Side-drum The side-drum has a small cylindrical shell, or hoop, with parchment stretched over both ends. Over the lower end there are 'snares' (gut or wire-wound strings stretched across, touching the parchment), which make a rattling sound when the drum is struck. On some side-drums the snares can be lifted clear of the parchment with a lever if the rattling sound is not required. Two wooden drum-sticks are used on the upper end of the drum. The

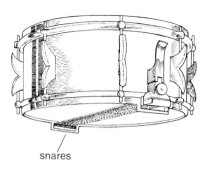

snares

Orchestral side-drum

side-drum is so called because it was slung at the player's side in military bands.

Bass drum   This is the largest drum and has a narrow, cylindrical wooden shell covered at both ends with stretched vellum. It has a deep, booming sound, which is produced by one stick with a large padded head. A single-headed bass drum with vellum over one end only is called a gong-drum.

Tenor drum   This is rarely used in the orchestra; it is midway in size between the side-drum and the bass drum.

Tambourine   This is a small wooden hoop covered over one end with stretched vellum. Pairs of small metal discs, called jingles, are inserted into the hoop so that they can vibrate freely when the tambourine is either shaken or hit with the knuckles or fingers of the player.

Triangle   This is a steel rod bent to form a triangle open at one angle. It is suspended by a piece of string, which is held in the performer's hand or attached to a music stand or to one of the drums. It is hit with a steel beater.

Cymbals   Cymbals are plates of brass fitted with leather handles in the centre. To produce different effects the two plates can be clashed together or rattled together at the edges, or one plate can be hit by any kind of drum-stick or brush. A pair of cymbals may also be mounted on a stand and clashed together mechanically, using a pedal.

Castanets   These came originally from Spain, and are two pieces of hard wood shaped like scallop shells. The two shells are hinged with a cord which is looped over the finger and thumb of the performer. Sometimes the two shells are hinged on a flat stick of hard wood and are sounded by shaking the stick. This type is used in the orchestra when there is no time for the player to loop a cord over his fingers.

Gong (tam-tam)   This is a large, heavy disc of metal with the edge bent, so that it looks like a dish. It is suspended on a string and is hit with a soft-headed drum-stick. Several gongs of different sizes and pitches may be used.

Other instruments of indefinite pitch used for special effects include the rattle, anvil, *Chinese block* and the whip, but these are rare.

OTHER INSTRUMENTS OF DEFINITE PITCH

Tubular bells   These are metal tubes of varying lengths hung on a wooden frame. There are usually

Celesta

eight (or more) forming a complete scale; a wooden mallet is used for striking them.

Celesta This is a set of steel plates, each of which is attached to a wooden resonator, and has an ethereal tone-quality. The sound is produced by hammers which are operated from a small key-board. Mustel invented the celesta in about 1880; Tchaikovsky introduced it in his 'Dance of the Sugar-Plum Fairy' in the *Nutcracker Suite*.

Glockenspiel This is a set of steel plates mounted on resonators and played with two small hammers like a dulcimer.

Xylophone This is a set of hard wooden bars arranged in the form of a piano keyboard and played with hammers in the same way as the glockenspiel.

THE ORGAN

The organ consists of a number of pipes of varying lengths mounted on a wind-chest and made to sound by wind, which is supplied to the wind-chest by means of bellows; in modern organs the wind supply is maintained electrically. Each pipe produces only one sound.

The organ is said to have originated in Chaldea and Greece, where the first organ-like instruments, the panpipes or syrinx, appeared. Reeds were cut off just below the knot, so that air blown down the reeds had to return to the open end. These were therefore stopped pipes producing a note an octave below that produced on an open pipe (see Chapter 1). By making a slit in the knot, and a notch with a bevelled edge in the pipe just above the knot, a sound could be made by blowing through the lower end of the reed. Thus the whistle (or 'flue') form of open pipe came into being. The reed pipe, though used in bagpipes in ancient times, was not used in the organ until the 15th century.

In the early organ the whistle pipes were placed on a wooden box, the wind-chest, and the wind was supplied by two people blowing through flexible tubes. Unless the pipes were stopped by the player's hands or fingers, all the pipes sounded together.

The slider was next introduced; each pipe was governed by a slider which was perforated, so that, on being drawn in or out, the wind to the pipe could be admitted or excluded. Next came a leather bag as a reservoir for the air, and later primitive forge bellows were used to supply the air.

The Roman *hydraulis* (or water-organ) came into being during the 3rd century BC. By using the weight of water, a steady wind-pressure could be maintained in the reservoir. Pipes were made of bronze and cop-

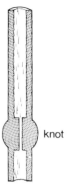

Cutaway diagram showing knot in a reed

knot

per. There is evidence of a water-organ in use during the 1st century BC; it had one and a half octaves, with keys and three ranks of pipes, and produced a 4-foot pitch.

The organ was used for public feasts, but was not adopted for use in the church until AD 450, when it was apparently used in Spain. In the 7th century it was used in Rome to help the singing of the congregation. The art of organ-making was known in England in the 8th century. In the 10th century there was a large organ at Abingdon Abbey and another at Glastonbury. Winchester Cathedral had a famous organ of 400 pipes of brass and copper. There were two organists; probably one worked the levers to make the pipes sound while the other worked the stop slides. Only one key at a time would have been used. The keys were three inches wide, and the organist was known as *pulsator organum* (organ-beater).

By the 14th century fixed organs came to be called

positive or positif, in contrast to portative (portable) organs, which were, by this date, being used in processions in Germany and Italy. The keys were closer together by this time and could be operated by the fingers of the player. By the end of the 15th century the organ was developing into its modern form, with two manuals and a pedal-board. By the 16th century pipes of conical construction were in use, and the keys were small enough for an octave to be spanned by the player's hand.

During the 18th century a section of the organ was enclosed in a box with a sliding front which allowed the tone to swell or diminish, hence the term 'swell-organ'. A marked development in the mechanism of the organ was made during the 19th century, whereby 'composition pedals', worked by the foot, enabled selected and fixed combinations of stops to be drawn. By developing the use of the pneumatic lever for operating heavy mechanism, larger organs were made possible. More recently, electric mechanisms have replaced the mechanical type, giving greater control with less effort and allowing the organist to concentrate on the musical effect.

Organ pipes are placed in rows or ranks, each rank supplying a complete range of notes of some particular tone-quality. So that all these ranks do not sound together, slides of wood pass under the tips of the pipes of each rank. When a particular rank is required, the slide controlling that rank is moved by the player pulling out a stop, so that holes bored in the slide coincide with the tips of the pipes.

Each note is fitted with a hinged lid, called a pallet, which seals the supply to the pipe until a key is depressed on a keyboard. When a key is depressed, either by the player's finger (on a keyboard, or manual) or by the player's foot (on the pedal-board), the pallet, connected to the key by a series of rods

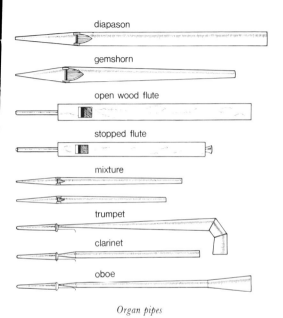

Organ pipes

'stopped' here means that the pipe is closed at one end by a cover or stopper; with its use the tone quality is changed, and the pitch is lowered about an octave. Flutes are of wood or metal and can be open or stopped. The bourdon, often a pedal stop, is a variety of stopped diapason. String-toned stops are usually made of metal and have thin bodies.

To acquire the exact tone-quality which is desired, subtle adjustments to the tone-producing portion of the pipe have to be made. This art of adjustment, known as voicing, is very skilled work and can be done only by experts.

There are many reed stops, which can imitate the tone-quality of orchestral reed and brass instruments (e.g. oboe, clarinet, trumpet). These different tone-qualities are produced by means of pipes of different scale—a term used to denote the difference in shapes and thicknesses of metal reeds.

Each manual of an organ is almost a self-contained organ and certain stops are associated with certain manuals. A large organ can have as many as five manuals.

The great organ is the basic manual, and has a diapason chorus of various pitches: 16 ft, 8 ft, 4 ft, 2 ft and a mixture.

The swell organ has reed as well as flue stops. The pipes are enclosed in a swell-box fitted with shutters which are worked by a pedal. When these shutters are opened the tone swells and when they are closed it diminishes. Nowadays a swell-box can be fitted to other manuals as well.

The choir organ has softer-toned pipes, and is often for accompanying.

The solo organ has stops comparable with solo orchestral instruments; these can be accompanied on another manual.

The echo organ is found on very large organs, and produces a distant, echoing effect on very soft pipes.

The pedal organ's notes sound an octave below that on the manuals. Its contribution to tone-quality is similar to that of the lowest-sounding orchestral instruments.

The specification of stops available on each manual varies with the size, make and location of the instrument.

Much of the organ is made of wood, which must

be of high quality. It has to be seasoned for many years so that it will withstand variations in humidity and temperature. If it is to be used abroad, it has to be specially treated so that it will withstand adverse conditions. The best material for the metal pipes is 'spotted metal'—a mixture of tin and lead; they are made from sheet metal, joined by very fine soldering. For the bellows high-quality sheepskin is used. Ivory and ebony are used for the manual keys. For the production of a first-class organ, as for any other instrument, only the best materials are used and highly skilled craftsmen are employed.

When an organ is required for a particular purpose, in a particular building, many factors have to be taken into consideration. Only after much thought and calculation can the required organ be designed; it is rare, therefore, for two organs to be identical.

Since 1930 the electronic organ has been in use; this has neither pipes nor wind, and it is claimed that many tone-qualities can be produced electronically. It occupies no more room than a grand piano, and is considerably cheaper than a pipe organ; its installation requires little more than connection to an electric power plug. The popularity of the pipe organ, with its subtlety and versatility, seems however to have been little affected by the electronic organ.

3   A BRIEF HISTORY OF
WESTERN MUSIC

BEFORE 1600

This was the age of choral music. Music in organized form began in the West with the spread of Christian worship.

SACRED MUSIC

Plainsong (1st–10th centuries) The words of the Catholic mass were chanted in free rhythm, with variations in pitch based on the ancient Greek modes, forerunners of our major and minor scales. The celebrants chanted alone and the choir sang in unison.

Organum (10th–12th centuries) Plainsong sung by a choir of boys and men in parallel 4ths, 5ths and octaves within comfortable pitch-range of their respective voices. 3rds and 6ths with some non-parallel movement were later added.

Conductus (12th–16th centuries) Two-part singing, with the tenor (the lower voice) singing the 'held' part (the *cantus firmus*, a phrase of plainsong in long note values), and the descant adding a florid part above.

80

Motet (13th–16th centuries) Originally the tenor sang the *cantus firmus* with the motetus and triplex (upper voices) adding faster-moving parts, sometimes to different words. Eventually the motet completely superseded the conductus and later a fourth voice was added. There is evidence from sculpture, paintings and literature that during the Middle Ages and the early Renaissance the singers' parts were doubled on instruments. One of the most prolific and inventive composers of motets in the 14th century was Guillaume de Machaut (d. 1377).

Some of the great polyphonic composers of the 15th and 16th centuries were Dunstable, Tallis and Byrd in England; Dufay, Josquin des Prés and Lassus in Flanders; Palestrina in Italy; and Vittoria in Spain.

It was in the later 16th century and early 17th (between *c.* 1570 and *c.* 1630) that most of the finest pure choral works were composed. The chief characteristics of this music are beauty and smoothness of melodic lines and counterpoint; dissonance is used sparingly and key definition is not yet completely established. Church music of this period was represented mainly by the mass and motet, and, in England after the Reformation, the Anglican service and anthem.

SECULAR VOCAL MUSIC

English composers were inspired to compose madrigals after becoming familiar with those of the Netherlands and Italy, particularly those published in London by Nicholas Yonge entitled *Musica transalpina* (1588). Contemporary love-poems, pastoral or fanciful verse, or poetry with classical allusions were set in several musical forms. The madrigal proper is similar in style to the motet for two to six mixed voices. Each phrase or line of verse is sung by one voice and taken up in turn by the others (through-composed). The ballet, for mixed voices, has a dance-like rhythm and often a 'fa-la' chorus, prob-ably originally for dancing. The music is repeated for each verse (strophic). The ayre is a solo song accompanied by other voices or by instruments (viols or lute). The music is repeated for each verse.

The Triumphes of Oriana (1603) is the most famous collection of madrigals published in England. It contains 29 madrigals written in praise of Queen Elizabeth I; all end with the refrain 'Thus sang the shepherds and nymphs of Diana, Long live fair Oriana.'

Some important madrigal composers of the period were Festa, Gastoldi, Gabrieli, Monteverdi, Maren-zio and Vecchi in Italy; Arcadelt, Philippe de Monte, Lassus and Willaert in the Netherlands; Hassler in Germany; and Byrd, Gibbons, Morley, Tomkins, Weelkes and Wilbye in England.

Italy was pre-eminent in music at this period; many English, Dutch, German and Spanish com-posers were trained there and held musical appointments there.

INSTRUMENTAL MUSIC

Although the doubling of vocal lines by instruments continued throughout the 16th century, purely in-strumental playing was gaining independence. Motets transcribed for the organ or for ensemble playing were written, called *ricercar* or *ricercare*. French chansons (gay, contrapuntal songs evolved from those of the troubadours and trouvères), which flourished to about the end of the 16th century, and other vocal works were similarly transcribed for in-struments and were known as *canzonas*. Some madri-gals were marked 'apt for voices or viols', and music identical in structure to madrigals was written for consorts of melodic instruments; these were called *fantasias* or *fancies*. When a variety of string and wind instruments were played together they were said to be playing in 'broken consort'.

Instrumentalists were rapidly developing technical skills, as is evident from contemporary instruction books and compositions for the viola da gamba, recorder and lute. Dances with variations and divisions (variations) on a ground bass (a simple repeated bass melody) were numerous. Toccatas for the virginals, harpsichord and organ were composed to show off a player's technical skill.

THE SEVENTEENTH CENTURY

Vocal music   In the 1590s a new art form, opera, was devised in Florence by a group of poets, musicians and artists. Accent and poetic metre were to be preserved, and the inflections of the voice were to enhance the expressiveness of the text. This kind of music is called recitative. Several operas, all based on the story of Orpheus and Eurydice, were produced: those by Peri and Caccini in 1600 in Florence, and *Orfeo* by Monteverdi in 1607 in Mantua.

They all contained, apart from recitative, beautiful phrases of music, more expressive of emotions and ideas, out of which grew the aria. Melodic lines were expanded with ornaments, runs, trills and shakes, to add more colour to the dramatic situations. Monteverdi gathered a large number of instrumentalists to accompany the singers and to add musical effects relevant to the drama, such as Orfeo's descent to the underworld; in his orchestra in 1607 there were viols, lutes, harps, a flute, trumpets, cornetts, harpsichords and organs of various sizes.

Opera required a clear, harmonic accompaniment (simple, three-note chords or triads) to support the solo voices. Music was made to match the sense of the words by musical punctuation (called cadences), and simple key relationships became clearly established. The demands of recitative brought about the use of the **figured bass**, a keyboard part with only the bass line in musical notation and the chords to be played shown by numbers that indicate the intervals of their notes above the given bass. The accompanist, being familiar with this musical shorthand, would 'realize' his part in an appropriate style from the harmonic information given and support the soloist as required.

This new, operatic style of writing was adopted, by composers of sacred music, notably Carissimi (1605–74), who used it for setting sacred texts in a dramatic style; this was the beginning of the oratorio.

Alessandro Scarlatti (1660–1725), Carissimi's most gifted pupil, established the 'da capo' **aria** form in his gay, brilliant operas. There were public opera houses, as well as private ones, in Rome, Naples and Venice, and to entertain a more popular audience these tuneful songs became the order of the day. These arias were in the nature of contemplation, the repeat of both music and words temporarily delaying the progress of the plot.

Instrumental music Scarlatti began his operas with an orchestral overture of three movements or sections: a fast one, a slow one and a dance usually a giga; this form of overture came to be known as the Italian overture. The orchestra was usually composed of strings, with an occasional wind instrument. The harpsichord alone accompanied recitatives.

One of the most famous societies of poets, musicians and artists met at the house of Cardinal Ottoboni in Rome. One of its members, **Arcangelo Corelli** (1653–1713), the first great violinist, devoted his life to performing on and composing exclusively for the violin and the violin family. He greatly extended the technique of string playing and founded an important school of violinists who followed both his playing and composing principles. His sonatas were for one or two violins and cello, with the harpsichordist playing from a figured bass.

Two types of **sonata** were common at this time. The *sonata da camera* ('chamber sonata'), often synonymous with the suite, usually has movements derived from the earlier court dances, such as the allemande, courante, sarabande and gigue, and often begins with a prelude. All the dance movements are in binary form with two musical sentences, each repeated, the first moving away from the original key, the second returning to it towards its close. All the movements are usually in the same key, with the possible exception of the sarabande.

The *sonata da chiesa* (church sonata) frequently played during church ceremonies is more serious in character; the movements bear only speed indications, although they contain the elements of dance forms. Their order is normally slow, fast (usually fugal), slow, fast (often in the rhythm of a giga). Instrumentation was similar to that of the *sonata da camera*, the organ possibly replacing the harpsichord. Works for one violin, cello and keyboard are called solo sonatas; those for two violins, cello and keyboard trio sonatas.

The *concerto grosso: da camera* and *da chiesa* are similar in form to the sonatas, but some have five movements. There are two groups of instrumentalists, one consisting of solo players (the concertino), the other a larger, accompanying group (the ripieno); both are accompanied by the harpsichord (playing from a figured bass). Corelli's *Christmas Concerto* is an example of a *concerto da chiesa*.

In the concertos of **Giuseppe Torelli** (1658–1709) and **Antonio Vivaldi** (*c.* 1678–1741), the solo group plays more brilliant music and often has its own themes, thus creating greater contrast with the ripieno group. Vivaldi introduced wind instruments and reduced the number of movements to three: fast, slow, fast. J. S. Bach later transcribed for harpsichords some of Vivaldi's concertos, retaining the original themes but adding richer harmonies and lively inner parts.

Vivaldi was the first important composer of the solo concerto for violin. This has three movements—fast, slow, fast or very fast. Basically it is like the *concerto grosso*, with the solo violin replacing the concertino section in the first and third movements. The second movement is often like an operatic aria, the violinist playing long, song-like phrases with light accompaniment. A cadenza is frequently introduced to exhibit the soloist's technical skill.

FRANCE

Vocal music   For many years mascarades, or masques, had been very popular in Paris. These elaborate entertainments, in which King Louis XIII himself enjoyed taking part, contained acting, dancing and singing. In 1656 Monteverdi's pupil, Cavalli, performed his own operas (in Italian) in Paris. The French enjoyed them, but considered they could produce better ones themselves.

Lully (Lulli) (1632–87), Italian by birth, French by adoption, spent all his working life at the court of Louis XIV, eventually gaining monopoly of opera production in France from 1672 until his death. He was a brilliant composer, but he could be selfish, scheming and unscrupulous, and his activities hindered any other musical development in France. His subjects for operas range from Greek drama to medieval romances which he treated dramatically through song, dance and spectacle. All his operas begin with an overture.

Instrumental music   The type of overture commonly used in French opera (later known as the French overture) consisted of a slow introduction, often with a dotted rhythm much copied by later composers, followed by a quick movement and concluding with a slow coda. The orchestra was becoming standardized: a basic string section was supplemented by wind, and by kettle-drums when required for special effects, and the harpsichord accompanied throughout. Lully 'conducted' audibly by beating with a long pole on the floor.

François Couperin (1668–1733), organist to the private chapel of the palace at Versailles, composed many suites of dances for the harpsichord. These **ordres,** showing influence of Lully's style, were delicate and beautiful; they were not intended for dancing. They often included movements entitled Courante, Sarabande, Gavotte, Menuet and Gigue. To some movements he gave fanciful names; in others he described hopefulness, ardour, langour and other emotions, and in so doing he was leading the way to programme music.

GERMANY

Church music had been checked in its growth in the 16th century by religious disturbances. After Martin Luther published his protest against the teachings of Rome, there was no use for mystical choral music in Protestant worship. **Chorales** were used, hymns in German (rather than Latin) which could be understood and sung by the congregation and were based on old church tunes and folksongs. These chorales, which became very dear to German Protestants, were used as a basis of variations for keyboard and were the source of the organ **chorale prelude** form brought to perfection by J. S. Bach.

Heinrich Schütz (1585–1672) was appointed chief court musician to the Elector of Saxony in 1614 to reorganize both the secular and sacred music of the court on Italian models. In his four settings of the

Passion according to the Evangelists he broke away from the traditional Latin Passions with their plainsong and dramatic choruses. He set the German narrative and dialogue in free recitative with dramatic choruses for the crowd, thus creating completely original works and preparing the way for the Passions of J. S. Bach.

Dietrich Buxtehude (1637–1707), of Danish origin, a great organist at Lübeck and much revered by J. S. Bach, held concerts of sacred **motets** and **cantatas** with organ and other instrumental accompaniment. The words and melodies of the chorales formed the bases of these cantatas; these too paved the way for J. S. Bach. Elaborate organ works based on the chorale were composed by Buxtehude and others.

ENGLAND

The Puritan rule had suppressed cathedral services and had banned theatrical entertainment, but with the return of King Charles II in 1660 great changes were made in manners and life in London.

Sacred vocal When the services of the Chapel Royal resumed, a choir was formed and trained by Captain Cook, who had served in the army under Charles I. Many of his choristers became famous musicians. Among them were Michael Wise and John Blow, both born in 1648, Pelham Humfrey, who was sent by Charles II to study in France with Lully, and Henry Purcell (1659–95), the greatest of them all. Purcell's career spanned the reigns of Charles II, James II and William and Mary. He composed much music for the church, theatre and concert room, and chamber music for the private house; he also wrote solo songs, duets, catches, odes, cantatas and instrumental works.

Purcell wrote many **anthems**, some for soloists and chorus and others for chorus alone. The festival setting of the *Te Deum* and *Jubilate* in D (1694) is his most celebrated church composition, with its great variety of expression and rich, daringly original harmony. It is scored for voices, strings, trumpets and organ.

Secular vocal   Purcell also wrote **odes** for various occasions. His first was in 1683 for the celebration of St Cecilia's Day (22nd November), at a festival service in Stationers' Hall, London.

Although there was no opera in England before the 1650s, no play was considered complete without music and dance. Plays such as Shakespeare's *A Midsummer Night's Dream* were revived and rewritten so that a **masque** with ballet, singing and acting could be inserted, no matter how incongruous it might seem. A production of *Dioclesian*, a version of a play by Beaumont and Fletcher, was advertised as 'being in the manner of an opera by Purcell'; he had written the incidental music and inserted a masque in the last act. His *Fairy Queen* (1692) is another example.

Purcell wrote one real opera, *Dido and Aeneas* (1689), for the pupils of Josiah Priest, a fashionable dancing-master in Chelsea. Purcell's music for this tragic love story begins with a French overture. Dido's song of lament, 'When I am laid in earth', written in the form of variations over a ground bass, is probably some of the most pure and moving music ever written by an English composer.

Instrumental music   Purcell's chamber music falls into two main categories: **fantasies** for viols, in an early, highly contrapuntal style associated with the Elizabethans; and **sonatas** in the Italian style. He wrote only one sonata for one violin and continuo, the *Sonata da chiesa* in G minor.

THE EARLY EIGHTEENTH CENTURY

One of the great Baroque composers, Handel, a German, dominated the musical scene in London. He settled there in 1712 after his first visit in 1710 (when he produced his first opera, *Rinaldo*).

George Frideric Handel (1685–1759), born in Saxony, became a proficient violinist, harpsichordist and composer by the age of 18. When he was 21 he studied in Italy with Corelli, Domenico Scarlatti and other musicians, many of whom he met at Cardinal Ottoboni's house. He was much influenced by these musicians, with the result that much of his music is italianate in its ideas and style.

Opera   Handel used the formalized Italian style in his operas: there were six principal characters, each having a specified number of arias to show off his or her technical skill, mostly in *Da capo* form; recitative was used for the development of the plot; and a chorus was occasionally introduced.

Handel brought the art of Italian opera to a climax in England. He employed foreign musicians, both singers and instrumentalists, who not only performed in opera but appeared at public concerts in and around the capital. London became so overtaken by foreign musicians that English music suffered lamentably for many years after Handel's death. Handel's operas were popular in England for some time. The English, though not understanding Italian, enjoyed the sumptuous presentation and spectacle and the vocal gymnastics of the singers, whose desire for adulation and applause became more important than the musical content of the opera.

Oratorio   During Lent when opera was banned, Handel produced his oratorios (*Saul, Israel in Egypt, Judas Maccabaeus, Messiah* and others), all on biblical subjects. He had the great gift of stirring listeners' emotions by the simplicity and directness of his music. In his oratorios, which were set to English words, Handel's genius gained its full power, and reached its zenith in *Messiah*. He created a work of such immediate appeal that its popularity still survives. His other choral works include cantatas, serenatas, anthems and other ceremonial pieces, many for the Duke of Chandos.

Instrumental music   As well as the major and minor choral works mentioned above, Handel also wrote suites, sonatas, concertos, occasional music and organ music.

The orchestra, in Handel's day, consisted basically of strings with two flutes (initially recorders, later transverse flutes), two oboes, some brass for special effects and kettle-drums. He conducted from the harpsichord.

Opera in English was revived in London in 1728 with the ballad opera *The Beggars' Opera*. A play with incidental music, this was an immediate success, but contributed to the eventual failure of Handel's operatic venture. The libretto, in English, by John Gay was a political satire on contemporary low life in London. Dr John Pepusch, a London music teacher, based his music on popular tunes and well-known ballads.

GERMANY

Johann Sebastian Bach   (1685–1750), another great Baroque composer, indeed one of the greatest composers of all time, was born in the same year as Handel. In his day Bach was known as the supreme performer on the organ, harpsichord and clavichord.

Violin
and viola
with bows

PLATE 1

Cello
with bow

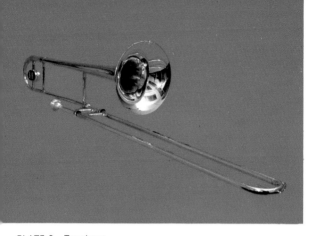

PLATE 2   Trombone
Cornet and trumpet

Tuba

PLATE 3

Triangle,
side-drum
with sticks,
castanets
and
tambourine

PLATE 4   Lute by Malteo Sellar, Venice 1637. Baryton by
Jacanes Saiprae, Berlin c. 1720. Hurdy-gurdy, French,
second half of 18th century. Octave spinet, c. 1600;
the notes sound an octave higher than printed

Guitar
attributed to
Jacob Stadler
c. 1625.
The ivory strips
on the back are
finely decorated

PLATE 5

Treble, tenor
and bass viols
with treble viol
bow

PLATE 6
Spinet made
by Johannes
Hitchcock,
London *c.* 1750
Reputed to have
belonged to
Handel

PLATE 7　Harpsichord attributed to Johannes Ruckers 1634, in the Long Gallery of Ham House, Surrey

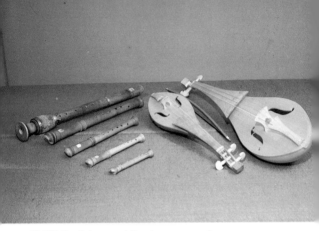

PLATE 8   Rebecs and Renaissance recorders

Crumhorns and a rackett

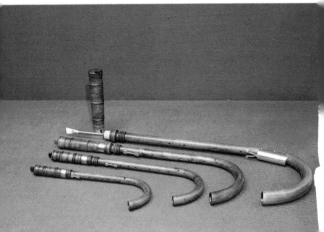

He wrote in every musical form of his day except opera, but the greatness of many of his compositions was not generally known or appreciated until their revival during the 19th century by Mendelssohn and Samuel Sebastian Wesley. His output sums up all the styles, devices and expression of the Baroque.

Bach's compositions relate closely to his various musical appointments. His organ works and cantatas were written during the period 1707–17 when he was court organist and chamber musician to Duke Wilhelm Ernst of Saxe-Weimar. His secular instrumental music was composed during the years 1717–23 when he was master of the court chapel and chamber music to Prince Leopold of Anhalt-Cöthen. The larger church works for voices and instruments, including about 300 cantatas, the *Passions, the Mass in B minor*, the *Christmas Oratorio*, etc., were written during 1723–50 when Bach was Kantor (head of the song-school) of the Thomasschule, Leipzig, and organist and director of music of two principal Leipzig churches.

Church cantatas   Bach's cantatas, each lasting about 25 minutes, were the main music of the Lutheran church service. Their words, relevant to each particular Sunday of the church calendar, consist of recitative, arias, duets and simple chorale settings for congregational singing. Bach's music is more deeply expressive than that of his predecessors; solo instruments interweave with the solo voices adding new tonal effects, the arias are generally more elaborate and deeply felt and the harmonies are more arresting.

Passions, Christmas Oratorio   In these works more stress is laid upon the gospel stories. The narrative words are sung in recitative by the tenor Evangelist and those of the Saviour (in the *St Matthew Passion* always accompanied by sustained strings) are sung by the bass. The words of the crowd are sung by the chorus, and all the other characters have distinctive solo parts. The music is highly dramatic, and in the *Passions* and in Part I of the *Christmas Oratorio* the story is interrupted for comment on its significance for the Christian with reflective arias expressing the deepest emotion. Bach's genius is evident throughout the *St Matthew Passion*: to take one example only, his five settings of the Passion chorale 'O Sacred Head surrounded' show the increasing gloom of the narrative; he reserved the lowest register of the voices for the last setting, which immediately follows Christ's death on the cross.

Mass in B minor　　This is Bach's most monumental work. In 1733, unhappy at Leipzig, he sent a petition to the Catholic Elector of Saxony asking for his powerful protection. With it he also sent the *Kyrie* and *Gloria* which he had specially composed. Later he completed the remainder of the Latin text of the mass, the *Credo, Sanctus* and *Agnus Dei*. This work takes three hours to perform and is regularly performed at Easter time in the concert hall.

In this work, in which Bach revealed his profound Christian faith, various styles are used. They include plainsong, of the style associated with Palestrina; the Italian aria, with florid vocal and instrumental passages; the ground bass; and the fugue. Bach used neither recitative nor chorale in the mass.

Instrumental music　　Most notable among Bach's instrumental music are his fugues, particularly 'The 48' (*The Well-Tempered Clavier*), a collection of two sets of 24 preludes and fugues which demonstrate that by tuning a keyboard instrument in equal temperament (slightly out of tune but acceptable to the ear) it was possible to play equally well in any of the 12 major and 12 minor keys.

Bach also wrote six French and six English **suites**,

based on French and Italian models of court dances, with much ornamentation; some have extensive preludes. His **toccatas** are brilliant rapid passages in free style, and his **chorale preludes** are organ works based on the chorales. In his **sonatas** for solo instruments—violin, viola da gamba and cello—he used elaborate melody, harmony and counterpoint without the support of an accompanying instrument. Bach also wrote trio sonatas for keyboard, violin, flute, etc.

Bach's **concerti grossi** were written for strings and other instruments. They include the famous six *Brandenburg Concertos*. He also wrote solo concertos.

In the *Goldberg Variations* for the harpsichord Bach gave each variation a definite character: the 16th is a complete French overture, and every third variation is in canon. Bach's works are based on the instrumental forms already in existence. He created no new ones, but in his *Art of Fugue*, a gigantic work, he demonstrated all the possible contrapuntal devices of his time with the greatest ingenuity, introducing in his final fugue the notes B, A, C, H as a signature. He died before completing the work.

ITALY

During the early 18th century there arose in Italy a school of violin playing which was to influence the rest of Europe.

Francesco Geminiani (1680–1761), a pupil of Corelli, was a great violinist and teacher. In his *Art of Violin Playing* he suggested, among other improvements, that the violin on the left side of the tail-piece should be held under the player's chin, giving a more comfortable hold. The angle of the violin was thus altered to give the bow equal command over all four strings. Also the hand was freed to allow the higher notes to be played by the fingers stopping the strings nearer to the bridge, which led to a more virtuoso style of playing.

Giuseppe Tartini (1692–1770), another great violinist, founded the Padua school of violin playing. He developed the art of bowing and increased the means of expressive playing by improving the structure of the bow. In his *Devil's Trill* sonata (supposed to be the outcome of a dream in which the Devil played to him) the music makes enormous demands on the player of both technical and interpretative skill.

Domenico Scarlatti (1685–1757), Alessandro Scarlatti's son, devoted his life to the harpsichord as a composer and performer. In his one-movement, short, glittering sonatas he extended the technique and individuality of harpsichord music: the player is required to use the full range of the instrument's keyboard and particularly to move the hands swiftly for wide leaps and sometimes to cross them over each other. The form of these short pieces is similar to the dances of the suite, namely binary.

THE CLASSICAL PERIOD

Carl Philipp Emanuel Bach (1714–88), J. S. Bach's third son, became court musician to Frederick the Great in 1738. His chief interest was playing and composing for the harpsichord. He had been trained by his father in various musical skills, but he felt he should explore new musical paths. He paved the way for the development of the classical form by using three movements to make a balanced composition: quick, slow, quick. The quick movements were extended and less contrapuntal than had been usual, with more use of accompanied melody.

Joseph Haydn (1732–1809) was born of humble Croatian parents. He learnt the violin and harpsichord when a choirboy in Vienna. After leaving the school he became accompanist to Porpora, a singing-teacher. In 1759 he was director of music to Count Morzin, and in 1760 accepted a similar post in the household of the Esterházy family at Eisenstadt, where he remained for 30 years. He composed music for the chapel and for plays, operas, chamber and orchestral music, also pieces for the baryton (see Plate 4), a kind of cello which his patron Prince Nicholas enjoyed playing.

After the Prince's death in 1790, Haydn, whose fame had spread through the many influential visitors to his patron's court, accepted an invitation by Salomon, a leading violinist in London, to visit England. He took six new symphonies with him which were performed there. He was also made a Doctor of Music at Oxford. He heard some of Handel's choral music in England, which was later to influence him. On his return journey to Vienna, Haydn met Beethoven in Bonn, which led to his teaching Beethoven composition and counterpoint until 1794. Haydn returned to England with another six symphonies for the Salomon concerts. He subsequently went back to Vienna, where in 1798 the first performance was given of *The Creation*, inspired by Handel's *Messiah*. Haydn died in Vienna in 1809.

Haydn's contributions to the development of the symphony (he wrote a total of 104) are most notable; he extended the three-movement Italian overture form to four movements by inserting the minuet and trio. For the minuet he used the binary form of the slow courtly dance (AABB), added a second minuet (CCDD) calling it a trio, and then returned to the first minuet AB (without repeats). This produced, therefore, a mixture of binary and ternary form. These movements are robust and lively and have the freshness of the open air.

Haydn was also one of the first composers to write a theme and variations movement as the slow movement of a symphony. He also modified the basic structure of sonata form as he wished, always with complete success. Some of his symphonies open with a short *adagio*.

First Movement SONATA FORM—*the basic formula*
Exposition: First Subject (Tonic)
Bridge passage—modulating (changing key) to lead into the
Second Subject or subjects in the key five notes above the Tonic, the Dominant key
Codetta (a little tail-piece)
Double bar—Exposition repeated.
Development of material in Exposition—passing through several keys, eventually returning to
Recapitulation: The First Subject in Tonic
Bridge passage (balancing that in Exposition)

Second Subject(s) in Tonic
Coda (enlargement of Codetta)

There are many variations on this formula such as:
(1) Development can be replaced by new material—this form is known as *Episodical Form.*
(2) In the recapitulation the First Subject can appear in the key five notes below the Tonic (the subdominant), in which case the recapitulation will appear as a complete transposition of the Exposition.
(3) Other variants can occur when the subject is in the minor key.

Taken as a whole, Haydn's varied and individual symphonic output is a landmark in 18th-century orchestral music.

Haydn's orchestra was basically a string orchestra, with two each of the woodwind family, two horns, two trumpets and one kettle-drum. For the last of his symphonies he increased his orchestra to 40 players. In his middle and late symphonies he abolished the continuo harpsichord, allowing the strings and bassoons to support the bass line on their own.

Haydn's earliest chamber works were outdoor music, written through necessity, for the price of a meal: serenades and divertimenti, mostly for violins, violas and string bass. They contained at least five movements, often with two minuets, and a slow movement for the leader to exhibit his virtuosity. From these early works the string quartet for two violins, viola and cello developed. At this time the trio sonata was still in vogue—Haydn's 40-odd quartets are an extension of that genre; they are similar in form to his symphonies and are completely self-sufficient. All these works were composed for skilled, sensitive musicians. They are immensely important in the history of chamber music, as they laid the foundations of string quartet composition throughout the 18th and 19th centuries.

Wolfgang Amadeus Mozart (1756–91) was born in Salzburg. He was an infant prodigy with the most remarkable musical gifts. At the age of six he and his 10-year-old sister toured the courts of Europe with their father, a professional musician, receiving much praise wherever they went. Later Mozart was made a member of the Archbishop of Salzburg's household, where he was treated badly and eventually thrown out. In Vienna, supported by the emperor and many members of the nobility, he gained much esteem as a composer of dramatic works. At the age of 25 he married. He suffered much deprivation and poverty during the remainder of his life; he died in Vienna aged 35, and was buried in a pauper's grave.

Mozart had the good fortune to have a friend in Joseph Haydn who taught him much about the art of composition. Mozart matured young, he refined both musical style and forms in his short life, so that Haydn learned from him in later life. This is very evident in Haydn's last 12 Salomon symphonies.

Mozart did little to modify musical form as he found it, but he exploited it to the full. With his phenomenal mastery of the technique of composition, especially his outstanding facility in contrapuntal writing and his subtle use of chromaticism, he infused his music with his innermost feelings. Often in his most lighthearted music one is aware that he is near to tears.

Mozart was the first to compose and play **concertos** for the piano and to explore some of its resources. The transition from the harpsichord to the piano took place as more expression (without mechanical aids) was demanded by composers. Mozart's keyboard writing is much less 'fussy' and much more lyrical than that of his predecessors, who were writing for the harpsichord. He composed between 40 and 50 concertos for solo instrument and orchestra, 31 for pianoforte, four for violin, and others for flute, harp, horn, clarinet and bassoon; he also wrote one for violin and viola.

The scheme of solo instrument alternating with the orchestra was abandoned: Mozart wrote for a solo instrument accompanied by the orchestra. He used the cadenza to give an opportunity for the solo performer to exhibit his technical skill; this is played unaccompanied near the end of a movement and usually ends with a trill as a signal for the orchestra to play again.

Christoph Willibald von Gluck (1714–87) was born in Bavaria, and died in Vienna. His parents belonged to the household of Prince Lobkowitz in whose castle he spent his childhood. He went to a Jesuit school, studying classics and learning the violin, harpsichord and organ. Later he had singing lessons and learnt the cello in Prague. Gluck joined Prince Melzi's band in 1736 in Milan, where he completed his studies in harmony with Sammartini.

After composing operas which were performed in a conventional style, in Italy and London, Gluck turned against the traditions of Italian opera on hearing Rameau's operas in Paris. He decided to revert to 17th-century principles, and stated his proposals for a 'reformed' style in the famous preface to his opera *Alceste* (1767). Briefly they were as follows: the overture should be a preparation for the opera; the music should enhance the sentiment of the words; the progress of the opera should not be interrupted by unnecessary vocal display or repetition; instrumentation should have relevance to the dramatic situation; there should be less distinction between recitative and aria; the work should have a noble simplicity of expression; and there should be no display of technical skill to detract from the drama. Gluck's best-known opera, *Orpheus and Eurydice* (1762), is still performed today.

Ludwig van Beethoven (1770–1827), born in Bonn, was the son of a poor musical family. He received his musical education from Neefe, the Elector of Cologne's chief court musician in Bonn. At the age of 13 he became Neefe's unpaid assistant as harpsichordist and conductor. At 17 he was sent by the elector to study with Mozart for three months. In 1792 Beethoven settled in Vienna and had lessons from Albrechtsberger and Haydn. No longer in the service of the elector, who recognized him as a great pianist and later as an even greater composer, he was financially dependent upon aristocratic amateurs. He never married nor did he have a settled home life. He suffered greatly from ill-health, from deafness which eventually became total and from much anxiety and sorrow occasioned by his ne'er-do-well nephew, who was his ward. He had a fine nature and found solace and inspiration in Nature and the countryside. His boisterous sense of humour, as well as the heights and depths of the human spirit with its passions and tenderness, are conveyed in his music with the utmost mastery.

His works include symphonies, overtures, concertos, sonatas, chamber music, choral music and one opera, *Fidelio*. His greatest contribution was his development of the expression of the profoundest thoughts and sentiments in purely instrumental terms.

His compositions fall naturally into three distinct periods: those up to 1800; those from 1800 to 1815; and those from 1815 to 1827. In the first period Beethoven was much influenced by Haydn and Mozart. His First Symphony was composed before Haydn's death. In the second period he experimented and expanded form and technique, and was living through revolutionary times politically and artistically. In those 15 years he produced his next seven symphonies. *The Choral Symphony* (no. 9) belongs to his last period. In his early works Beethoven seems to belong to the 18th century, but he was a man ahead of his time, and his later works have much of the Romantic element within them.

Whereas Haydn wrote over 100 symphonies, and Mozart wrote over 40, Beethoven wrote only nine, but what is lacking in number is balanced by their stature and significance. His works are on a larger scale, and show the expansion of symphonic and sonata forms: the coda acts as a second development section so that the sonata form became four-fold; key changes (moving from one tonal point to another) became very daring; the range of tone-colour (the blending of instrumental sounds) was extended; and a larger orchestra was required.

In all his symphonies Beethoven used flutes, oboes, clarinets and bassoons as a complete woodwind section. In the first two symphonies he had two horns, two trumpets, kettle-drums and complete strings, which included the double bass. In the *Eroica* (no. 3) he added a third horn. In the Fifth he added the piccolo, double bassoon and three trombones in the final movement. In the Ninth he introduced a vocal quartet, chorus, triangle, cymbals and a fourth horn. In all his symphonies Beethoven made use of the woodwind section as an orchestra in itself, independent of the strings. In the *Eroica*, and all that followed, he gave the violas and double basses independence and expanded his writing for the lowest strings as well as for the bassoon and kettle-drums.

In his 32 piano sonatas Beethoven introduced phrases reminiscent of orchestral instruments, e.g. horns, flutes, strings, etc. He used sonorous chords and low bass notes which sound rich and clear, and extended well into the upper registers of the keyboard. All his piano music is dramatic and expressive, particularly that of his last years, which is highly original.

Franz Peter Schubert (1797–1828) was born in Vienna. His family were intensely musical, and their string quartet playing was much admired locally. At the age of 11, Schubert entered the royal choir school where he received good general and musical education. On completing his studies at 17, he taught in his father's school, but left after a short while to devote all his energies to composition with the help of his elder brother and friends. In 1818 he had a regular post as music teacher to the daughters of Count Johann Esterházy, a younger member of the family of Haydn's patrons. He was a torch-bearer at Beethoven's funeral in 1827 and in the following year was buried in Vienna beside him.

Schubert composed his first six symphonies before he was 21. His style of composition is akin to that of Haydn and Mozart, but all his symphonies have the individuality of his particular melodic and harmonic genius. Best-known among his symphonies are the Eighth, *The Unfinished*, with only two movements, and the Ninth, known as *The Great C major*.

Through Beethoven's playing and compositions the pianoforte had become recognized as a very expressive instrument. Schubert, inspired by the lyrical romantic poems of Goethe, Heine and others, composed over 600 songs (**Lieder**) with piano accompaniment. With his highly imaginative use of harmony, modulation and rhythm he created moods, scenes and atmospheres of dramatic intensity, always with apt piano accompaniment. He incorporated some of his songs into his string quartets, e.g. *The Trout* and

Death and the Maiden. With this highly expressive form of chamber music Schubert paved the way for Schumann, Brahms, Hugo Wolf and Richard Strauss, who were associated with the German **Lied** in the 19th century.

THE ROMANTIC PERIOD

With the symphonies of Beethoven and Schubert the Classical period reached its climax. These symphonies opened the way to the Romantic period. They expressed in musical terms the most profound human feelings with a directness of communication such as is found in Romantic literature and painting. Music had always contained some quality of romance, however small, but at the end of the 18th century the romantic element became predominant. The Romantic movement, affecting all the arts, spread over Europe, particularly to France and Germany, and influenced English literature (e.g. the works of Sir Walter Scott and William Wordsworth). Nationalism, too, spread rapidly over Europe after the Napoleonic wars, and became especially strong in the second half of the 19th century.

OPERA

Carl Maria von Weber (1786–1826) established German national opera, based on German folk legends and history, with the libretto sung in German and set to music expressive of German tradition and temperament (e.g. *Der Freischütz*).

German legend also attracted **Richard Wagner** (1813–83). He used Beethoven's harmonic structures but extended their emotional content. In his later works he dispensed with the distinctive styles of individual operatic numbers intermingling recitative and song as the text demanded.

He adopted a new form of construction using significant musical fragments, 'Leitmotivs', to associate with each character, object or idea. He increased the dramatic intensity of the music through the announcement and development of Leitmotivs. He

compositions are disciplined harmonically by tonal centres rather than by conventional tonality, and his harmony has its roots in the traditional triads. Much of the music of the middle period of his life makes reference to Baroque and Classical forms and styles and is often termed 'neo-Classical'. The outstanding quality of his music is the use of compelling rhythmic patterns, jazz idioms, ostinati and conflicting rhythms in counterpoint. These devices will be heard in *The Firebird*, *Petrouchka* and *The Rite of Spring*. Stravinsky has had a considerable influence on the development of 20th-century music. Prokofiev and Shostakovich have made use of similar compelling rhythms and neo-Classicism, and the Frenchmen Francis Poulenc and Darius Milhaud, as well as the Americans Roger Sessions and Aaron Copland, show traces of Stravinsky in their works. In his desire to develop an American style of composition Copland adopted the rhythms, melodies and sonorities of the jazz idiom. Improvisation as used by jazz musicians began to be used with the traditional orchestra in the form of concertos during the 1950s and other jazz idioms have continued to have an effect on many 20th-century American composers.

OTHER DEVELOPMENTS

Arnold Schoenberg (1874–1951) was born in Vienna. He played the violin and cello, and began composing in his youth. Up to 1903 his compositions were in a late German Romantic style. Then he began experimenting with and expanding the chromatic element in his harmonies, and by 1908 he had begun composing atonal works. In so doing he laid the main foundations for 20th-century music. In his new style the structure of the music is a prime concern and the texture is often very bare.

In 1912 his *Pierrot Lunaire* appeared. This work for reciter/singer and instrumental group demands new techniques from the performers: the reciter/singer needs to use a style somewhere between speaking and singing; the strings have to produce *glissandi* after plucking the notes, and the woodwind have to use flutter-tonguing (rolling their Rs while blowing).

After a break Schoenberg began composing again in 1921 and turned his attention to the use of the 12-note technique. Schoenberg greatly influenced the music of two of his pupils, Alban Berg (1885–1935) and Anton von Webern (1883–1945).

Béla Bartók (1881–1945) was born in Hungary. He studied composition and was an outstanding pianist. He was much influenced in his composition by the works of Richard Strauss. In 1905 he became interested in Hungarian folk music which he began to collect, as did Kodály, his fellow-countryman. In 1906 they jointly published 20 folksongs with piano accompaniment.

Up to 1904 Bartók's harmonies were of the post-Romantic richness of Richard Strauss, and for the next two years he was attracted by Liszt's method of transforming thematic material. From 1906 he adopted the characteristics of his native folk idiom which included using old modes and also the pentatonic scale. He made much use of the descending interval of the 4th, and his rhythms were influenced by the accentuations of Hungarian language. His harmonies became more chromatic and he used bi-tonality (the use of two different keys in two simultaneous melodic lines). In 1925 his music adopted elements of the neo-classical style, which he combined with folksong idioms. Much of his large-scale music is very brilliant in its orchestrations.

Paul Hindemith (1895–1963), born in Germany, was a professional violinist and viola player, both a soloist and a player of chamber music. He introduced his own string quartets at various contemporary music festivals. He was also interested in early music, which he studied, and which he and his students performed on authentic instruments.

During the Nazi régime Hindemith went to Turkey, Switzerland and America, where finally he settled. In 1940 he became a professor at Yale University. Through his teaching and theories he had much influence on modern music both in the USA and in Europe. After the Second World War he taught at the University of Zurich, alternating this with his appointment at Yale. Later he devoted his time to composing and touring as a conductor.

In his sonatas, symphonies and concertos he returned to the foundations of Classical structures, though abandoning Classical tonality. He used harsh dissonances, very strong rhythms and he exploited chromaticism. He was very interested in amateur music-making and wrote a great deal of easily playable music.

THE ENGLISH RENAISSANCE

Ralph Vaughan Williams (1872–1958) is considered to be the founder of the 20th-century English national school of composition. After going to Cambridge University he studied with Charles Stanford and Hubert Parry at the Royal College of Music, with Max Bruch in Berlin and later with Ravel in Paris. At the turn of the century he became involved in research into English folk music, collecting much material on his travels round the country. His own music was considerably influenced by his researches, and also by the music of Elizabethan composers: this is evident in his use of modes, his gently flowing melodies and his contrapuntal style. He wrote much choral music, both sacred and secular, orchestral and ballet music, symphonies, concertos, film music, opera, chamber music and songs.

Vaughan Williams, together with Gustav Holst, Edward Elgar, William Walton and many other English composers, is recognized as having established the 'English Renaissance' which was to grow to full maturity with the music of Benjamin Britten and Michael Tippett.

Benjamin Britten (1913–76) was born in Suffolk. After studying piano with Harold Samuel and composition with Frank Bridge whilst at school, he entered the Royal College of Music, continuing piano lessons with Arthur Benjamin and composition with John Ireland. He was in America for part of the Second World War, returning to England in 1942. He then settled in Suffolk.

In 1947 he founded the English Opera Group and in 1948 started the Aldeburgh Festival. He was a brilliant pianist and conductor as well as being an outstanding composer, writing both for professional musicians, from whom he demanded great technical skill, and for amateurs and children. He wrote much music specially for his friend, the tenor Peter Pears, and for many other artists, including Rostropovich, the famous Russian cellist, and the mezzo-soprano Janet Baker. One of the most outstanding features of Britten's music is his sensitive, expressive handling of English texts for solo and choral voices. The compositions of Richard Rodney Bennett, Gordon Crosse, Nicholas Maw and many others show Britten's influence.

While in the Soviet Union and elsewhere in eastern Europe a nationalistic style of writing is encouraged, many musicians in western Europe and the USA have been influenced by the traditional music of the East. Claude Debussy was fascinated by Javanese music, which he heard at the Paris Exhibition in 1899; Gustav Holst was very interested in Asian music and in Sanskrit, which he learnt, and he translated Sanskrit texts into English for some of his choral works. Stravinsky, Rimsky-Korsakov, Bartók and Olivier Messiaen were all influenced by Eastern music, and in their various ways absorbed some of its characteristics.

Oriental music is characterized by subtlety and variation of individual sounds, and their interrelationships, a great variety of pitch relationship (infinitely greater than that in Western music), and elaborate rhythms and polyrhythms, unfettered by the bar-line and the straitjacket of harmonic structures.

The adoption into Western music of oriental scales or modes containing different intervals from those of Western music have contributed greatly to harmonic development. The fusing of East and West has already brought great changes to Western music, both in sounds and musical structure. Conventional instruments are required to produce new sounds, and conventional, oriental instruments are introduced into traditional Western music.

THE ELECTRONIC AGE

The invention of the vacuum tube at the beginning of the century made possible the electronic organ, in which the notes of the harmonic series are created artificially and so blended to produce notes of various qualities which are inherent in the conventional pipe organ. From these beginnings the whole electronic system has grown.

Electronic music was begun in 1948 in France by Pierre Schaeffer, a radio producer and engineer. Electronic studios were set up in many parts of the world. The first efforts at so-called compositions consisted of collages, in which sounds of everyday things, such as engines, birdsong, street noises, etc., known as **musique concrète,** were combined with sounds produced by musical instruments. From these early experiments the many processes of electronic music have been developed.

Today **electronic music** is produced on most elaborate equipment and requires highly technical skill on the part of the composer to use it. The term electronic music implies that the performance is live, i.e. it is actually being performed by the composer and players manipulating knobs, switches and other controls on electronic apparatus before an audience.

Tape music on the other hand, implies an assemblage of pre-recorded sounds of both conventional instruments, possibly electronically modified, combined with sounds produced totally electronically, all of which may be superimposed on tape—a long process in the laboratory or studio.

Of the contemporary composers who have made significant use of electronic techniques, the most important include Pierre Boulez (b. 1924), also well known as a conductor, and Karlheinz Stockhausen (b. 1928), a pioneer in electronic techniques, who was much influenced by the American John Cage (b. 1912). Others who have used these techniques are the Frenchman Edgar Varèse (1885–1965), the Italian Luigi Nono (b. 1924), the Hungarian György Ligeti (b. 1923) and English composers such as Harrison Birtwistle (b. 1934) and Roger Smalley (b. 1943).

4 MUSICAL TERMS IN COMMON USE

Abendlied (Ger.): Evening song.
Abendmusik (Ger.): Evening music.
A cappella (It.): Literally, in church style. Unaccompanied vocal music.
Adagio (It.): Slow.
Air and variations: Usually a song-like melody, which is followed by a repetition of itself with varied melody, harmony or rhythm.
Albumblatt (Ger.): Literally, album leaf. A short light instrumental piece, usually for the keyboard.
Aleatory music: Music in which sounds are arranged in a haphazard way (as with the throwing of a dice) introducing elements of chance with regard to both composition and performance.
Allegretto (It.): Rather quick, but usually slightly slower than allegro.
Allegro (It.): Literally, lightly and brightly. Now usually means quickly.
Allemande (Fr.), **Alman** (Eng.): A moderately lively dance in four-beat time. Generally the first or second movement of 17th- and 18th-century dance suites.
Andante (It.): Walking pace.
Andantino (It.): Originally meant slower than

andante, but has come to mean quicker than andante.

Answer: in the exposition of a fugue, the name given to the main theme when it appears in the dominant key in answer to the subject in the tonic.

Anthem: A piece for church choir with or without solos, accompanied or unaccompanied, sung during the Anglican church service, but not forming part of the liturgy. It is also sung in other English-speaking Protestant churches.

Arabesque (Fr.): A term used by, among others, Schumann and Debussy for pieces containing ornamental melodic figures originally applied to Arabic and Moorish architectural ornamentation.

Aria (It.): A song or air. A, B, A. There are many such arias, usually in three sections, in 18th-century operas and oratorios. See **Recitative.**

Atonal music: See **Serial music.**

Aubade (Fr.), **Morgenmusik** (Ger.): Morning music, usually instrumental but sometimes vocal.

Ayre (Old Eng.): A 16th- or 17th-century song with melodic interest mostly in the top part, often applied to a solo song with lute accompaniment, or to a purely instrumental piece, for viol consort.

Badinage, Badinerie (Fr.): A light, playful 18th-century instrumental piece in quick duple time.

Bagatelle (Fr.): A short piece, usually for piano, humorous or light in character.

Ballad opera: See **Opera.**

Ballade (Fr.): A romantic type of piano piece having a narrative quality; a term first used by Chopin to describe certain of his piano pieces.

Ballet music: Music for a stage entertainment consisting entirely of dancing.

Ballett, Ballet (Old Eng.): a 16th- or 17th-century choral piece, similar to a madrigal but lighter and more dance-like in rhythm, often with a 'fa-la' chorus.

Barcarolle (Fr.): A song or instrumental piece in the style of a boat-song, e.g. Offenbach's *Barcarolle*.

Basse danse (Fr.): A 14th- to 16th-century French dance, in which the dancers' feet were kept close to the ground.

Basso ostinato (It.): Literally, obstinate bass. See **Ground bass.**

Bergerette (Fr.): A short, pastoral song, usually associated with 18th-century Classical French style.

Bolero (Sp.): A lively Spanish dance, often with castanets in triple time. See **Seguidilla.**

Bourrée (Fr.): Originally a French 17th century peasant dance in quick duple time, with every phrase beginning on an upbeat; often used as one of the livelier movements of a suite.

Branle (Fr.), **Brawl** (Eng.): An old French dance, from the old French word *branler* (to swing from side to side).

Caccia (It.): Chase or hunt; in music, strictly, a canon, usually vocal, in which the parts appear to 'chase' each other.

Cachucha (Sp.): An energetic solo Andalusian dance in triple time.

Cadenza (It.): A passage introduced near the end of a song or instrumental piece for the performer to display his technique; particularly common in a concerto.

Canon: A piece of music consisting of one melody which is begun in one voice or part and continued in that part while it is begun in another, thus becoming interwoven with itself (canon two in one). A third voice (canon three in one), and more, may enter in the same way; the round *Three Blind Mice* is a form of canon.

Cantata (It.) : A short secular or sacred work for solo voices or choir, usually with orchestral accompaniment.

Canzona (It.) : A part-song or instrumental piece in madrigal style, but lighter in character and simpler in construction.

Capellmeister (Ger.) : See **Kapellmeister.**

Capriccio (It.), **Caprice** (Fr. and Eng.) : A short, lively piece often of a humorous or capricious nature.

Cavatina (It.) : A melody, sung or played, in the style of a simple short song, particularly common in opera.

Cebell: An early English gavotte, but rather quicker.

Chaconne (Fr.) : Originally a slow triple-time dance, but now often a set of variations on a ground bass. See **Ground bass**.

Chamber music: A term applied to concerted music for a small number of players or, more rarely, singers, with one performer to each part.

Choral (Ger.), **Chorale** (Eng.) : A traditional German Lutheran hymn-tune.

Chorale prelude: A type of organ piece mainly used in German churches in 17th and 18th centuries to introduce and elaborate the hymn to be sung by the congregation.

Classical music: a term used to distinguish art music from popular music; also used to refer to music of the Haydn–Mozart–Beethoven era as opposed to that of the Baroque or Romantic eras.

Clavier: See **Klavier.**

Coda (It.) : Literally, tail; a finishing passage or section at the end of a piece or movement.

Comic opera: See **Opera.**

Concert overture: See **Overture.**

Concerto (It.) : Literally, a performance in concert.

(1) **Concerto grosso** (It.) : A work for two groups of instruments playing in concert and answering

each other; the larger group is called *ripieno* (full) and the smaller, often soloists, *concertino*.

(2) **Classical concerto:** A work for one or more solo instruments and orchestra, demanding brilliance and virtuosity from the soloists; usually in three movements.

Concertstück (Ger.): See **Konzertstück.**

Consort: An old English word meaning instruments playing together, such as a consort of viols; 'broken consort' signifies instruments of more than one type playing together.

Continuo (It.): Figured bass, Thorough bass. A form of shorthand, whereby figures placed over or under the bass in a keyboard part show what harmony is to be filled in by the player. In an orchestral work, the given bass would normally be doubled by the lower strings.

Contrapuntal music: Music made up of melodies combined simultaneously in such a way that the resultant harmony is satisfying and the music is flowing rather than progressing in blocks of chords.

Contredanse (Fr.): An English country dance, performed with the couples facing each other.

Counterpoint: See **Polyphony.**

Czárdás, Csárdás (Hung.): A Hungarian dance in duple time, with two movements: Lassu (slow) and Friss (quick).

Da capo (It.): From the beginning.

Divertimento (It.), **Divertissement** (Fr.): A light orchestral work, primarily for entertainment, either made up of a string of popular melodies, or containing a number of contrasting movements similar to a suite, but longer. In French stage music *divertissement* means a set of varied dances or instrumental pieces that are incidental to the plot.

Divisions: A 17th-century English term for a particular type of variation that involves breaking the long notes of a melody up into shorter ones.

Double (Fr.): An old French name for a type of variation that involves embellishment, common in the 18th-century dance suite.

Duet, Duo: A composition for two voices or instruments of equal importance with or without accompaniment, or for two players on one instrument, as for example in a piano duet.

Dumka (Russ.; plural **dumky**): A Russian or Czech lament, usually instrumental, with alternating slow and animated sections.

Duple time: Two beats in a bar.

Ecossaise (Fr.): A dance of Scottish origin; now applied to a lively piece in duple time of the country-dance type.

Entr'acte (Fr.): Originally any music played between parts of a play or a musical work; later applied to short concert pieces.

Etude (Fr.): Literally, a study; an instrumental exercise in technique and/or expression.

Extemporization: See **Improvisation.**

Fancy, Fantasy: 16th- and 17th-century polyphonic chamber music, generally consisting of several correlated sections, performed without a break.

Fandango (Sp.): A lively Spanish dance in triple time, accompanied by guitar and castanets; there may be intervals during which the dancers sing.

Fanfare: A trumpet flourish.

Fantasia (It.), **Fantasie** (Fr.), **Fantasy** (Eng.): Either a character piece, often for piano, of the Romantic period; or a composition based on themes from opera, folksongs, or popular tunes. See also **Fancy.**

Farandole (Fr.): A Provençal processional dance,

in 6/8 time, performed to the accompaniment of pipe and tabor.

Figured bass: See **Continuo.**

First movement form: See **Sonata form.**

Folia, Follia (It.): Originally a wild Portuguese dance; one particular tune was very popular among composers of the 17th and 18th centuries, who wrote many variations on it over a ground bass.

Fugue: A polyphonic piece with a fixed number of melodic parts or voices. It is based on a short theme called a subject which is introduced by each voice in turn, often alternating in tonic and dominant keys according to the voice (see **Answer**). Each voice then continues its own line as the others enter in turn until all voices have made one entry. After this *exposition* further entries of the original subject are made between freer passages, called *episodes*. Many ingenious modifications of the subject may be made, such as augmentation (spacing it out in longer note values), diminution (squashing it into smaller note values) or inversions (turning it upside down). Other devices used are stretto (making the entries of the subject tumble in on each other more quickly) and pedal (sustaining one note, usually the bass, during the progress of the other parts).

Galliard, gagliarda (It.): A lively triple-time dance, which in a dance suite often followed the *pavane* and often contained the same music in different rhythm. Paired pavanes and galliards were popular in the 15th and 16th centuries.

Galop: A vigorous duple-time round dance, popular in the early 19th century.

Gavotte: A quadruple-time dance with every phrase beginning on the third beat; often one of the lively movements of the suite.

Giga (It.), **Gigue** (Fr.), **Jig** (Eng.): A lively dance form usually in 6/8 or 12/8 time, often appearing as the last of the movements of the suite.

Giocoso (It.): Humorous, cheerful, playful.

Giojoso (It.): Joyful.

Glee: A secular part-song intended to be sung by a choir and very popular in 19th-century England; the main melodic interest is in the top part and the music is repeated for each verse.

Gopak, hopak: A lively duple-time Russian dance.

Grand opera: Opera without spoken dialogue. See **Opera.**

Grave (It.): Solemn.

Grazioso (It.): Gracefully.

Gregorian chant: See **Plainsong.**

Ground bass: A short phrase in the bass which is repeated many times with variations built above it.

Habanera (Sp.): A Cuban dance in moderate duple time which became popular in Spain; the name comes from the word Havana, the Cuban capital.

Hammerklavier (Ger.): Literally, hammer-keyboard; an obsolete 19th-century term for the piano.

Harmony: The sounding together of musical notes of varying pitch.

Hopak: See **Gopak.**

Hornpipe: An old English dance, originally triple time, later in duple or quadruple time, associated with sailors; it gets its name from the wind instrument that accompanied it.

Humoreske, Humoresque: A short instrumental piece, humorous or capricious in character; a well-known example is Dvořák's *Humoresque.*

Idyll: A short instrumental piece of a quiet, fanciful or pastoral character; an example is Wagner's *Siegfried Idyll.*

Impromptu (Fr.): Literally a short extemporized

piece, but often applied to short instrumental compositions, usually for the piano.

Improvisation: The art of composing music while performing it; also used to describe pieces which are free in style and sound as if they are improvised.

Incidental music: Music performed during or in connection with a spoken play, as, for example, Grieg's incidental music to Ibsen's *Peer Gynt*.

Interlude, Intermède (Fr.): See **Entr'acte.**

Intermezzo (It.): A short piano or orchestral piece. See also **Entr'acte.**

Interval: The distance in pitch between two notes; the name of each interval (e.g. 2nd, 3rd, 4th, etc.) reflects the number of notes of the major or minor scale that it covers; for example, C to D is a 2nd, C to E is a 3rd, C to F and E to A are 4th. The smallest normal interval in Western music is the semitone (or minor 2nd), e.g. C to D flat. See the plan of the piano keyboard on pages 174 and 175.

Intrada (It.): See **Overture.**

Invention: A term used for a type of short contrapuntal keyboard piece, made famous by J. S. Bach's pieces; a short melodic phrase is announced and a whole composition is developed or invented from it.

Jazz: A type of 20th-century popular music, originally coming from the USA about 1914 and owing much to social dancing and negro influence. The development of special rhythm patterns, syncopation and unusual sound effects both in orchestration and chord progressions are some of its main features.

Jig: See **Gigue.**

Jota (Sp.): A rapid triple-time dance from northern Spain, performed with castanets.

Kapellmeister (Ger.): Master or director of music

in the establishment of a German prince, nobleman or high ecclesiastic, who was responsible for all the music in concert-room, opera house and chapel; one of his duties was to compose for court occasions.

Key: (Readers should refer to the plan of the piano keyboard given at the end of the book.) The main note, or tonal centre, to which all the notes of a composition relate, is the keynote, or tonic, and the relationships of the other notes to this determines the character, or quality, of the key. There are two main qualities of key, major and minor. As an example, play from C to C on the white notes on the piano. This constitutes the scale of C major, with the semitones between the third and fourth notes, E and F, and the seventh and eighth, B and C. Play it again, but instead of E play E flat. This produces the ascending form of C minor, with the semitones between the second and third and the seventh and eighth notes. The distance from C to E flat is a 'minor 3rd', hence the terms 'major' and 'minor'. Similar scales can be built from any note; the first note is the keynote and the others constitute the notes of that key.

Keynote; See **Key.**

Kinderstück (Ger.): A children's piece.

Klavier (Ger.): Originally any sort of keyboard instrument; now the modern German word for 'piano'.

Köchel: See **Opus.**

Konzertstück (Ger.): A short type of concerto, sometimes found as a title on piano music meaning for concert performance.

Ländler: An Austrian triple-time dance, from which the waltz was developed.

Langsam (Ger.): Slow.

Largo (It.): Slow and stately.

Lebhaft (Ger.): Lively.

Leger or **Ledger:** Short lines above or below the

stave to show notes which are too high or too low to be written upon it.

Leitmotiv (Ger.): A short theme, or group of notes, associated with an idea, object or person which re-appears at appropriate moments. The device was made famous by Wagner's operas; it had been used also by Mozart, Weber, Berlioz and others.

Lento (It.): Slow.

Lesson: See **Suite.**

Libretto: The text of an opera or other dramatic work.

Lied (Ger.): Song.

Lied ohne Worte (Ger.): Song without words; a title for a type of short, lyrical piano piece made famous by Mendelssohn.

Madrigal: A composition for several voices, poly-phonic in style, usually secular, and with words of a higher literary value than many other contemporary forms of secular vocal music. Originally a 14th-century Italian term, it more commonly refers to the secular vocal works of the 16th and early 17th centuries in Italian and English.

Maestoso (It.): Majestic.

Marcia, Alla (It.), **Marziale** (It.): In the style of a march.

Mascarade (Fr.): A masked ball, or music associ-ated with it or suggesting it. Originally it was the French equivalent of the English masque.

Masque: A lavish stage entertainment in the 16th and 17th centuries, indulged in by the nobility, and one of the predecessors of opera. Music, poetry, scenic effects, dancing and action were important features of it.

Mass: The celebration of the Eucharist, or Last Sup-per, in the Catholic liturgy; a musical setting of it is also called a mass.

Mazurka or **Mazur** (Polish): A triple-time Polish national dance from the 16th century or earlier, which reached a high point in the 18th and 19th centuries. The second beat tends to be accented. Chopin composed a number of piano pieces in this form.

Meno (It.): Less.

Minuet, Menuet (Fr.), **Minuetto** (It.), **Menuett** (Ger.): A triple-time French country dance, which was modified by the court of Louis XIV towards the end of the 17th century, from whence it rapidly became popular throughout Europe. In this more graceful, modified form it was sometimes used in dance suites, and it frequently became part of the classical sonata. In the sonatas and symphonies of Haydn and later composers, the *minuet's* character changed, becoming quicker and livelier, and in some of Beethoven's works it is often replaced by a Scherzo. Often there is a second minuet, termed the trio. See **Trio**.

Mixed voices: A choir or an ensemble with both male and female voices.

Moderato (It.): At a moderate speed.

Modulation: A change of key within a piece or movement.

Molto (It.): Much, very.

Moment musical (Fr.): A title favoured by Schubert for some of his piano pieces; also a fanciful name for a short instrumental work.

Morgenlied (Ger.): See **Aubade.**

Mosso (It.): Movement; *più mosso* means faster, *meno mosso* a little slower.

Motet: A sacred work for voices, usually unaccompanied; also may be applied nowadays to a secular work of the same type.

Moto (It.): Motion.

Moto perpetuo (It.): Perpetual motion.

Musette (Fr.): The name for the French bagpipes,

which is also applied to a dance with a drone-bass, often found in the 18th-century dance suite.

Nachtmusik (Ger.): Literally, night music; a piece of music for light entertainment, such as a serenade.

Nachtstück (Ger.): Literally, night piece, or nocturne.

Nocturne: A short instrumental piece, often for piano, which became popular in the 19th century through the music of John Field and, more notably, Chopin.

Nonet: A work for nine performers.

Notturno (It.): See **Nocturne.**

Novelette: Literally, a short story; a title for short piano pieces of a Romantic character, much used by Schumann.

Obbligato (It.), **Obligat** (Ger.): A solo instrumental part, which is of outstanding importance in a work, is said to be an obbligato, i.e. compulsory or obligatory. (Sometimes the word is incorrectly spelt **obligato**.)

Octet: A work for eight performers.

Opera (It.): A staged, dramatic work sung with orchestral accompaniment.

Opera, Ballad (Eng.): A light, farcical English stage work with spoken dialogue, often parodying grand opera; the most famous example is *The Beggar's Opera* (1728).

Opera buffa (It.): Comic opera: Opera on a comic subject, usually with spoken dialogue.

Opéra comique (Fr.): A term used to include most French opera with spoken dialogue whether or not it is on a comic subject.

Opera, grand: Opera without spoken dialogue.

Opus (Lat.): Literally, work. A term used from the

17th century onwards, abbreviated op., to show the chronological position of a work in a composer's output; thus 'op. 1' would signify an early work and 'op. 101' a later one. Opus numbers are not always a reliable guide however, because they normally refer to publication rather than composition. 'Op. posth.' (*opus posthumous*) is a work published after the composer's death. For several composers (e.g. Haydn, Schubert) other numbering systems may be used in addition to or in place of opus numbers. For Mozart's works the Köchel (K) numbering system is used (compiled by Ludwig von Köchel in 1862 and subsequently much revised).

Oratorio (It.): A sacred opera without action; Handel used the term also for secular works.

Ordre (Fr.): See **Suite.**

Ostinato, Basso ostinato (It.): Literally, an obstinate (i.e. repetitive) bass. See **Ground bass**.

Overture: An opening instrumental piece for an opera, oratorio, suite, play, or other work. An overture that is habitually played at a concert, severed from the work to which it originally belonged, or one composed as an independent piece, is known as a 'concert overture' (e.g. Mendelssohn's *A Midsummer Night's Dream* and *The Hebrides*).

Partita (It.): See **Suite.**

Part-song: A vocal piece for several voices, with or without accompaniment, particularly popular in the 19th century.

Passacaglia (It.), **Passacaille** (Fr.): See **Chaconne**.

Passepied (Fr.), **Paspy** (Eng.): A triple-time dance similar to a minuet, but usually more spirited.

Passion music: The story of Christ's Passion set to music, usually for solo voices, chorus and orchestra.

Pastorale: A rustic piece, often associated with

shepherds' pipes or bagpipes, sometimes with drone-bass, usually in 6/8 or 12/8.

Pavane, Pavan: A slow, duple-time stately dance popular in the 16th century; it was often paired with the galliard. A modern work based on the pavane is Ravel's *Pavane for a Dead Infanta*.

Perpetuum mobile (Lat.): **Moto perpetuo.**

Phantasy: See **fantasy**.

Phrase: A small group of notes, comparable to a clause in prose, more or less complete in itself; a number of phrases make a musical sentence.

Piano quartet: A work for piano and three strings.

Piano quintet: A work for piano and four strings.

Piano trio: A work for piano and two strings.

Più (It.): More.

Plainsong: Ancient traditional liturgical song, sung in unison and free rhythm, and still used as the main musical part of the services of many liturgies, both Christian and non-Christian.

Polka: A lively, duple-time couple dance from Bohemia, originating in the early 19th century.

Polyphony: A number of melodic parts which are combined to make musical sense. See **Counterpoint**.

Postlude: A piece played after a ceremony.

Prelude, Praeludium: An introductory piece in no particular form played either before an instrumental fugue or as the first movement of a suite. See **Overture.** Also a title for a short instrumental piece.

Prestissimo (It.): Very quickly.

Presto (It.): Quickly.

Programme music: Music which tells a story in sound, particularly in the 19th century.

Quadruple time: Four beats in a bar.

Quartet: A piece for four performers.

Quintet: A piece for five performers.

Recitative: Declamation in song, with fixed notes but flexible speech-rhythms; often used to provide the connecting narrative link between the arias in an opera, oratorio, cantata or other work.

Requiem: A mass for the dead.

Rhapsody: An ecstatic type of instrumental composition, first popularized by Liszt.

Rigadoon (Eng.), **Rigaudon** (Fr.): An old Provençal dance in duple or quadruple time.

Ripieno (It.): Literally, full. (See **Concerto.**)

Ritornello (It.): A short, recurring instrumental passage, particularly common in an aria or concerto when the soloist is silent.

Romance (Eng.), **Romanza** (It.): A short, song-like instrumental piece.

Romantic music: Music with strong, expressive feeling, a term normally applied to music composed during the 19th century; comparable, and almost contemporary with the Romantic schools of literature and painting.

Rondeau (Fr.), **Rondo** (It.): A piece in which the main tune appears at least three times, interspersed between other episodes.

Rondino (It.): A short piece in the form of a Rondo.

Rubato, Tempo Rubato (It.): Literally, robbed time; for purposes of expression in some compositions, the performer hurries over some notes, and lingers over others (thus robbing some to pay others).

Ruhig (Ger.): Peacefully.

Saltarello (It.): A lively dance with leaps. In various collections of 16th-century dance tunes it is the second of two dances sharing the same tune, the first in common time, the second in three-beat time. It was also a popular Roman dance in 3/4 or 6/8 time.

Sarabande (Fr.): Originally a slow solo court dance in triple-beat time, with an accent frequently on the second beat; it is found in 17th- and 18th-century suites.

Scale: Notes of a key arranged in ascending or descending order, e.g. C major: C D E F G A B C. See also **Key**.

Scherzo (It.): A joke; a humorous type of movement which often replaced the minuet in sonatas and symphonies by Beethoven and others; also an independent instrumental piece, usually for piano.

Schnell (Ger.): Quickly.

Scordatura: The mis-tuning of the violin such as is demanded for the solo violin part in the opening bars of the *Danse macabre* of Saint-Saëns.

Score: A full copy of the music of a work as distinct from a part, in which the individual performer has only his own music written out. A score showing all the parts of a vocal and orchestral work is known as a full (or conductor's) score. A copy showing all the instrumental parts of an orchestral work is known as an orchestral score. A copy of a choral work giving all the voice-parts over a piano arrangement of the orchestral accompaniment is known as a vocal score.

Seguidilla (Sp.): An old Spanish dance in quick triple time; probably introduced into Spain by the Moors, it has much in common with the bolero, but it is much faster. A feature of the dance is its sung passages, called *coplas*. Castanets are always used.

Septet: A composition for seven performers.

Serenade, Serenata (It.): Evening music, vocal or instrumental, also a light, entertaining instrumental work for chamber group or small orchestra in several movements.

Serial music: Primarily, a term used to describe 20th-century music composed on the 12 notes contained within the octave, arranged as the composer chooses; no note may recur until all 12 have been sounded, either singly (melodically) or in clusters (harmonically), and all 12 are of equal importance.

Sevillana (Sp.): A local type of seguidilla.

Sextet: A work for six performers.

Siciliana (It.), **Siciliano** (It.), **Sicilienne** (Fr.): A Sicilian pastoral dance, in a moderate 6/8 or 12/8 time; found in sonatas and suites.

Sinfonia (It.): In the 18th century, an overture, or an instrumental piece in a vocal work; Bach also used the term in some of his keyboard works.

Sonata (It.): Originally music sounded, or played, as distinct from cantata, music sung; the title has been given to different types of work but in the Classical period it described a substantial work for one or two instrumentalists, normally in three or four movements.

Sonata form, first movement form: A form frequently used for single movements (not always first movements) of sonatas, symphonies, concertos and chamber works. There are three main sections in the movement: the Exposition, which introduces the main thematic material of the movement; the Development, which expands and develops the thematic material; and the Recapitulation, which restates the material (often with coda). The element of contrast (between themes and keys) is an important feature of this form.

Sonata rondo form: A musical form combining elements of both sonata form and rondo form.

Sonatina (It.): A work shorter and simpler than a sonata.

Song without words: A title used by Mendelssohn for a number of his short, lyrical pieces.

Sostenuto (It.): Sustained.

Ständchen (Ger.): See **Serenade**.

Streichorchester (Ger.): String orchestra.

String quartet: A work for four stringed instruments—first and second violins, viola and cello.

String trio: A work for three stringed instruments—violin, viola and cello.

Subject: A theme, such as appears in a fugue or in sonata form.

Suite: An instrumental work made up of a number of dance movements all in the same key. The early 18th-century suite usually consisted of pieces in the following dance forms: *allemande*, *courante*, *sarabande* and *gigue*; sometimes it opened with a prelude, and other dances such as *gavottes*, *passepieds* and *bourrées* were included. The title is also applied to more modern works consisting of several movements but lacking the formality of sonata structure. Other names used for pieces similar in design to the suite are *Ordre* (Fr.), *Partita* (It.) and *Lesson* (Eng.).

Symphonic poem: A large Romantic work for orchestra in one movement with a 'programme', introduced by Liszt and developed by Richard Strauss; also called 'tone poem'.

Symphonic variations: Theme and variations for orchestra, sometimes also requiring an instrumental soloist.

Symphony: Literally, sounding together. The word has been used at different periods in different ways; from the Classical period onwards, it describes a large-scale work for orchestra, usually in three or four movements, one or more of which may be in sonata form.

Tarantella (It.), **Tarantelle** (Fr.): A quick dance in 6/8 time; supposed to be a cure for tarantism, a disease caused by the bite of the tarantula spider, found around Taranto in Italy.

Tempo (It.): Time.

Tempo giusto (It.): Strict time.

Tempo rubato (It.): See **Rubato**.
Ternary form: Three-fold form. See **Aria**.
Terzetto (It.): A piece for three performers; a trio.
Theme: An air, melody or other musical idea that forms the basis for a piece of music.
Thorough bass: See **Continuo**.
Toccata (It.): A title given to rapid and brilliant keyboard pieces.
Tone poem: See **Symphonic poem**.
Tordion (Fr.): An old Basque dance in triple time.
Transposing instruments: To simplify the notational and technical difficulties involved in playing some instruments, their music is written in a key other than that in which it is intended to sound. The clarinet player in an orchestra has two instruments, one in B flat and the other in A: when he sees the written note C he associates it with a certain fingering, which when used on the B-flat instrument produces the note B flat, and on the A instrument produces the note A. If, therefore, the composer wishes the player to sound the note C on the B flat instrument, he must write the note D (a whole tone higher). Similarly, for the A instrument to sound C he must write the note E flat (a tone and a half higher than the sound he requires), because the note produced will sound a tone and a half lower than written. Horns, trumpets and clarinets are the chief transposing instruments.
Trepak: A Russian dance similar to the *gopak*.
Trio: (It.): A work for three performers; also used to mean a second minuet (or in later works a second *scherzo*) between the minuet or scherzo and its customary repeat. Sometimes these movements were written in three-part harmony, hence the name.
Triple time: Three beats in a bar.
Triplet: Three notes played in the time of two.
Tutti (It.): Literally, everyone. A direction for

everyone to play as opposed to 'solo' in a concerto, or as an alternative to 'divisi', when one string section in an orchestra plays more than one part instead of playing in unison.

Un poco (It.) : A little.

Variations: Varied treatments of a given theme. See **Air and variations**.
Villanella (It.) : A 16th-century type of part-song that originated in Naples; it is usually lighter than the serious madrigal and sometimes parodies it.
Vivace, Vivo (It.) : Lively.
Vorspiel (Ger.) : Overture or prelude.

Wiegenlied (Ger.) : Cradle-song.

Zapateado (Sp.) : A fierce Spanish dance in triple time, accompanied with stamping instead of castanets.
Zigeunerlied (Ger.) : Gipsy song.
Zingaro, Zingara (It.) : Gipsy (male and female).
Alla Zingarese, in gipsy style.

5   COMPOSERS: BIOGRAPHICAL NOTES

RCM—Royal College of Music
RAM—Royal Academy of Music
RMCM—Royal Manchester College
of Music, now the Royal Northern
College of Music

Albeniz, Isaac (1860–1909) b. Camprodón, Spain. After an adventurous career as a pianist he studied composition with d'Indy and Dukas, and was influenced by Debussy in Paris. *Works:* mostly operas and piano music.

Arne, Thomas (1710–78) b. London. Went to Eton and studied at Oxford University. Leading British composer of his day. *Works:* operas, songs, instrumental music and incidental music to plays.

Arnold, Malcolm (1921–   ) b. Northampton, England. Studied at the RCM with Gordon Jacob. *Works:* Symphonies, concertos, film scores, ballets and chamber music.

Babbitt, Milton (1916–   ) b. Philadelphia, USA. Trained as a mathematician but later studied music. He extended the 12-note system and serialism beyond Schoenberg and Webern. *Works:* chamber music, songs and electronic works.

Bach German family of musicians. The most famous were:

   Bach, Johann Sebastian (1685–1750). See page 92.

   Bach, Carl Philipp Emanuel (1714–88) J.S. Bach's second surviving son. See page 97.

   Bach, Johann Christian (1735–82) J.S. Bach's youngest son. He spent most of his life directing operas and concerts in London. Appointed Music Master to Queen Charlotte, wife of George III. Known as the 'English' or 'London' Bach. *Works:* operas, symphonies, etc., vocal and chamber music.

Balakirev, Mily Alexeievich (1837–1910) b. Nizhny Novgorod, Russia. Founder of 'The Five' (Russian composers who pursued professions other than music: Borodin, Cui, Mussorgsky, Rimsky-Korsakov). Glinka had inspired him with the idea of Russian nationalism. *Works:* piano music, songs (slightly oriental) and other instrumental works.

Banks, Don (1923–) b. Melbourne, Australia. Taught by Seiber and Dallapiccola, also influenced by Babbitt and the jazz idiom. Is involved with various musical associations in London, dealing with new music and electronic music, etc. *Works:* instrumental music for films and television, songs, chamber music.

Barber, Samuel (1910–) b. Philadelphia, USA. Studied at Curtis Institute, Philadelphia, later taught piano there. His music is based on traditional forms and style with some anchorage in tonality. *Works:* stage, choral, orchestral, military, chamber and ballet music, songs.

Bartók, Béla (1881–1945) b. Nagyszentmiklós, Hungary. Also an outstanding pianist and a folksong collector. Studied at the Budapest Academy of Music. He helped to develop a Hungarian national style of music by introducing folksong into classical forms.

Much of his music is dissonant and highly coloured. *Works:* stage, orchestral, choral, chamber and piano music.

Bateson, Thomas (1570–1630) English composer, and organist of Chester Cathedral, later of Christ Church Cathedral, Dublin. He was famous for his madrigals.

Beethoven, Ludwig Van (1770–1827) b. Bonn, Germany. See page 102.

Bellini, Vincenzo (1801–35) b. Catania, Sicily. Studied at the Naples Conservatory. A popular opera composer who gave the singers every opportunity to show their charm and technical skill.

Bennett, Richard Rodney (1936–) b. Broadstairs, England. Studied at RAM, London, with Lennox Berkeley and Howard Ferguson, later in Paris with Pierre Boulez. His works include much 12-note music. *Works:* operas, film scores, orchestral and chamber music, songs.

Berg, Alban (1885–1935) b. Vienna. Studied with Schoenberg. See page 162. *Works:* operas, *Wozzeck* and *Lulu*, also chamber and orchestral music, songs.

Berio, Luciano (1925–) b. Oneglia, Italy. He studied in his home town and later in Milan. From 1963 to 1971 he was resident in the USA and returned to Italy in 1972. He is one of the few avant-garde Italians to have achieved a truly international status. Much of his music is serial, and his vocal music, some of which was written for his wife, the soprano Cathy Berberian, is particularly successful.

Berkeley, Lennox (1903–) b. Oxford, England. Educated at Oxford and in Paris. Much of his music is in a traditional style. *Works:* oratorio, ballet, chamber and piano music, etc.

Berlioz, Hector (1803–69) b. La Côte-St-André, France. Awarded the Prix de Rome by the French

France and was later named People's Artist of the Soviet Republic. Was originally influenced by 'The Five'.

Glière, Reinhold (1875–1956) b. Moscow. Studied in Kiev and at the Moscow Conservatory, later in Berlin. Held important posts in Kiev and Moscow and toured extensively as a conductor. Was a popular and much honoured composer of Romantic, nationalist compositions. *Works:* symphonies, chamber music, ballet, songs and piano pieces.

Glinka, Mikhail (1804–57) b. nr Smolensk, Russia. Learnt the piano with John Field. Spent some time in Italy, hearing much Italian opera, and returned to Russia and composed operas. He was recognized as the father of the Russian Nationalist School and founder of the Romantic Movement in Russia.

Gluck, Christoph Willibald von (1714–87) b. Erasbach, Germany. Was sent to a Jesuit school in Bohemia, then studied in Prague. He had lessons in singing, organ, harpsichord and violin, and later the cello. He earned a living by playing the violin for the peasants' dances and singing in church. See page 101.

Goehr, Alexander (1932–) b. Berlin. Came to England in 1933. Studied at RCM, then in Paris with Messiaen and Yvonne Loriod. He founded the Theatre Ensemble to perform his works and has held several university posts. He uses serialism and repetitive motifs with dramatic force and virtuosity.

Goossens, Sir Eugène (1893–1958) b. London. A member of a famous musical family, he studied at the RCM with Charles Wood and Stanford. Was a violinist in the Queen's Hall Orchestra (1912–15) and conducted orchestras in Britain, the USA and Australia. *Works:* operas, orchestral, chamber music and songs.

Gounod, Charles François (1818–93) b. Paris. Studied at the Paris Conservatoire and won the Prix minster, London. He was chorister of the Chapel Royal, and one of the greatest English composers. See page 89.

Quilter, Roger (1877–1953) b. Brighton, England. Educated at Eton and studied composition in Frankfurt. He is well known for his many songs, tunes for children's rhymes and incidental music to plays.

Rachmaninov, Sergey (1873–1943) b. Semyonovo, Russia. He studied at the St Petersburg and Moscow conservatories and left Russia in 1918 to live in Switzerland and the USA. He was one of the finest pianists of his day and the last great composer of late Romantic piano music; his concertos and works for solo piano are in an individual, lyrical style which is often highly emotional and sometimes melancholy.

Rameau, Jean-Philippe (1683–1764) b. Dijon, France. He was a son of the organist of Dijon Cathedral. He played the violin, organ and harpsichord. Being completely absorbed in music he was at first totally uneducated, but later rectified this. His writings on musical theory laid the foundation of the modern study of it. He was for many years a musician at Louis XIV's court. His many operas, ballets and harpsichord music greatly influenced French composers.

Ravel, Maurice (1875–1937) b. Ciboure, France. He studied with Fauré at the Paris Conservatoire and was awarded only the second Prix de Rome, as he was considered a 'dangerous, revolutionary composer'. He was however intelligent, witty and versatile, a typical product of French culture. *Works:* songs, piano, chamber, orchestral music, etc. See page 110.

Rawsthorne, Alan (1905–71) b. Haslingden, Lancashire, England. He trained at the RMCM as a cellist and pianist and was director of School of Dance-

his style o'
and taug
Angeles.
and piano
Schuber
page 104.
Schuller
to the Th
was self-t
known or
has explo
structure,
instrumei
Schuma:
many. H
literature
works of S
ist but da
composin
chamber
Schuma:
trained ai
held seve
the Juilla
Videocor
scale sym
can popt
opera, et
Schutz,
many. Se
Scriabin
was an ai
servatory
his piano
other orc
Searle,
At Oxfor

Mime, Dartington, Devon, and then a freelance composer. *Works:* mainly instrumental.

Reger, Max (1873–1916) b. Brand, Bavaria, Germany. He was also a pianist and organist and held many academic posts, including one at Leipzig Conservatory. His works, organ, piano, orchestra, chamber music and songs, are in a highly Romantic style.

Respighi, Ottorino (1879–1936) b. Bologna. He studied in Bologna, in Russia with Rimsky-Korsakov and in Berlin, and then settled in Rome as director of the St Cecilia Conservatory. His music is in a bright, melodious style, often with vivid and pictorial orchestration, and some works are in the neo-classical style. *Works:* stage, orchestral and chamber music, songs.

Rimsky-Korsakov, Nikolai Andreievitch (1844–1908) b. in the government of Novgorod, Russia. He was already composing at nine years. He entered the Royal Naval College, St Petersburg, and learnt piano and cello under difficulties. He was much influenced by Balakirev and was one of 'The Five'. *Works:* in Romantic tradition, for organ, piano, orchestra, chamber music and songs.

Rossini, Antonio (1792–1868) b. Pesaro, Italy. Both his parents were musicians. He studied at Bologna Conservatory. At 37 he had written 36 operas; after that he turned to sacred music. His melodic gifts, sense of humour and blending of instruments and voices have made many of his operas extremely popular.

Rubbra, Edmund (1901–   ) b. Northampton, England. A pianist, he studied at Reading University and at the RCM with Holst, Vaughan Williams and R. O. Morris. He was a senior lecturer at Oxford and a professor at the Guildhall School of Music, London. *Works:* instrumental, vocal, church music, etc.

early operas are rather melodramatic, but he later developed a more dignified style. His gift for melody and characterization and his sense of drama have helped to make his music extremely popular.

Villa-Lobos, Heitor (1887–1959) b. Rio de Janeiro, Brazil. He had little formal education and turned to playing the cello in cafés. He travelled throughout Brazil, became interested in folk music and began to compose. He studied in Paris on a government grant and later founded the Brazilian Academy of Music. He is recognized as an outstanding Latin American nationalist composer. *Works:* instrumental, ballet, piano, choral, etc.

Vivaldi, Antonio (*c.* 1678–1741) b. probably Venice. He was a violinist at St Mark's, Venice. After being a *maestro di cappella* in Mantua, he was made *maestro de' concerti* at the Ospedale della Pietà, Venice (a foundling hospital for girls), which had a fine orchestra and choir, and he remained there all his life. *Works:* operas, church music, various kinds of instrumental music. See page 86.

Wagner, Richard (1813–83) b. Leipzig. He came from a theatrical family and to the Thomas schule, Leipzig. He was the greatest German composer of Romantic operas in the 19th century. He built a theatre at Bayreuth, under the patronage of the King of Bavaria, for his many operas. See page 106.

Walton, Sir William (1902–   ) b. Oldham, Lancashire. He was a choirboy and later an undergraduate at Christ Church, Oxford. He was mainly self-taught, but had advice from Ansermet and Busoni. His witty *Façade,* an entertainment using Edith Sitwell's poems, brought him fame, and his orchestral music is becoming better known. *Works:* symphonies, concertos, choral, film, and chamber music, etc.

Warlock, Peter (real name Philip Heseltine) (1904–

30) b. London. He studied in Germany and at Oxford, and composed chamber music and songs. Under his real name, he wrote on Delius (with whom he had a lifelong friendship) and edited Elizabethan lute-songs. Much of his music reflects his interest in the supernatural.

Weber, Carl Maria von (1786–1826) b. Lübeck, Germany. He was the founder of German national romantic opera. He was also a pianist and studied in Salzburg with Michael Haydn (Joseph's younger brother), and in Vienna. After a dissipated life among royalty, actors and musicians he settled down. He was a great admirer of Beethoven, and much of his music reflects literary influences. He died in London after conducting his opera *Oberon* at Covent Garden. *Works:* much piano music, operas, orchestral and chamber music, songs. See page 106.

Webern, Anton von (1883–1945) b. Vienna. He studied at Vienna University and composed while still a child. He had lessons with Schoenberg in 1904. He conducted and travelled extensively in Europe. After about 1908 his style changed from tonal to atonal and he greatly developed and extended the principles of atonality. *Works:* operas, orchestral, choral and chamber music, songs.

Weelkes, Thomas (1575–1623) b. London. He was organist of Chichester Cathedral and was well known as a madrigalist and composer of sacred music. See page 82.

Wilbye, John (1574–1638) b. Diss, Norfolk, England. He served the Kytson family near Bury St Edmunds all his life, and was one of the greatest madrigalists. See page 82.

Williamson, Malcolm (1931–   ) b. Sydney, Australia. Composer, pianist and organist. Master of the Queen's Musick since 1975.

Wolf, Hugo (1860–1903) b. Windisch-Gräz, southern

Styria. He attended the Vienna Conservatory and later lived for four years in a small village near Vienna, where he wrote, feverishly, one song after another. He also wrote an opera and some instrumental music. He died, in an asylum, at the age 43. See page 105.

REVIVAL OF EARLY MUSIC

From the early years of the 20th century research into music of the past has steadily increased. Today performances of early music by both professional and amateur musicians are part of the musical scene. The demand for replicas of musical instruments has grown enormously; many craftsmen are engaged in making accurate reproductions of existing original instruments and re-creating (from the careful study of contemporary pictures and detailed descriptions) obsolete ones. For interested amateur instrument makers construction kits are available for purchase. The Fellowship of Makers and Restorers of Historical Instruments, whose aim is to promote authenticity in the making, restoration and use of such instruments, issues a quarterly bulletin to all its members. This contains information of both practical and research interest. Exhibitions of early musical instruments, sponsored by the Early Musical Instrument Makers' Association, are held biennially in London.

There is a very informative quarterly journal entitled *Early Music* (published by Oxford University Press, 44 Conduit Street, London W1R oDE); it is profusely illustrated with photographs and musical examples—a veritable treasure house of information for anyone interested in the subject. Apart from articles by experts, it contains music publishers' and instrument makers' advertisements, information about recordings of early music, notices of recitals, concerts, courses and exhibitions, and much other information. Its annual *Register of Early Music* is a worldwide directory of players, teachers and makers of early instruments.

Information on music festivals is usually published in the national newspapers and in music journals. Fuller details can be obtained direct from the secretary of the appropriate festival where its location is given in this list; enclosure of a stamped, addressed foolscap envelope is appreciated. The following list gives some of the more important music festivals in Great Britain and the Republic of Ireland; all are annual unless otherwise stated.

Aldeburgh Festival of Music and the Arts Aldeburgh, Suffolk (June)
Bath Festival Bath, Avon (May–June)
Birmingham Festival Birmingham (September)
Brighton Festival Brighton, Sussex (July)
Cardiff Festival Cardiff, Wales (March)
Cheltenham Arts Festival Cheltenham, Glos. (July)
Chichester see **Southern Cathedrals**
Dublin Festival Dublin, Ireland (January)
Edinburgh International Festival Edinburgh, Scotland (August–September)
English Bach Festival London (April–May), Oxford (May)
Gloucester see **Three Choirs**
Glyndebourne Festival of Opera Glyndebourne, Lewes, Sussex (May–August)
Harrogate Festival of the Arts Harrogate, Yorkshire (August)
Haslemere Festival Haslemere, Surrey (July)
Hereford see **Three Choirs**
Leeds Festival Leeds, Yorkshire (October; biennial)
Llandaff Festival Llandaff, Cardiff, Wales (June

INDEX OF MUSICAL INSTRUMENTS

Main entries are given in heavy type; plate references are in italics

178